THE

SECOND ADMINISTRATION

OF

JAMES MADISON

1813—1817

HISTORY OF THE UNITED STATES,

BY

HENRY ADAMS.

HISTORY

OF THE

UNITED STATES OF AMERICA

DURING THE SECOND ADMINISTRATION OF

JAMES MADISON

By HENRY ADAMS

Vol. III.

ANTIQUARIAN PRESS LTD.
New York
1962

First Published
1891-1896
by
Charles Scribner's Sons

———

Reprinted 1962
by
Antiquarian Press, Ltd.
New York, N.Y.

Edition Limited to 750 Sets

Library of Congress Catalog Card Number: 61-8054

Printed in the U.S.A.
———
NOBLE OFFSET PRINTERS, INC.
NEW YORK 3, N.Y.

CONTENTS OF VOL. III.

HISTORY OF THE UNITED STATES.

———◆———

CHAPTER I.

DURING the spring and summer of 1814 the task of diplomacy was less hopeful than that of arms. Brown and Izard with extreme difficulty defended the frontier; but Gallatin and Bayard could find no starting-point for negotiation. Allowed by Castlereagh's courtesy to visit England, they crossed the Channel in April, and established themselves in London. There Gallatin remained until June 21, waiting for the British government to act, and striving with tact, caution, and persistency to bring both governments on common ground; but the attempt was hopeless. England was beside herself with the intoxication of European success.

Although the English newspapers expressed a false idea of the general will, and were even at cross purposes with the Ministry in American matters, their tone was in some respects an indifferent barometer for measuring the elation or depression of the public temper, and exercised some influence, rather apparent than real, on the momentary attitudes of government. Had Castlereagh and his colleagues been really controlled by the press, no American peace could have been made. Whatever spirit of friendship for America might exist was necessarily silent, and only extravagant enmity found expression either in the press or in society.

Perhaps because ministers were believed to wish for peace with the United States, the London "Times," which was not a ministerial journal, made itself conspicuous in demanding war. The "Times" had not previously shown a vindictive spirit, but it represented the Wellesley and Canning interest, which could discover no better course than that of being more English than England, and more patriotic than the Government. The "Times" was always ably written and well edited, but its language toward the United States showed too strong a connection with that of the Federalists, from whose public and private expressions the press of England formed its estimate of American character.

The "Times" indulged to excess in the pleasure of its antipathy. Next to Napoleon, the chief victim of English hatred was Madison. For so mild a man Madison possessed a remarkable faculty of exciting invective. The English press surpassed the American Federalists in their allusions to him, and the "Times" was second to no English newspaper in the energy of its vituperation. " The lunatic ravings of the philosophic statesman of Washington " were in its political category of a piece with " his spaniel-like fawning on the Emperor of Russia.[1] . . . The most abject of the tools of the deposed tyrant ; . . . doubtless he expected to be named Prince of the Potomack or Grand Duke of Virginia." [2] The " Sun " somewhat less abusively spoke of " that contemptible wretch Madison, and his gang ; " [3] but the " Times " habitually called him liar and impostor.

" Having disposed of all our enemies in Europe," the " Times " in the middle of April turned its attention to the United States. " Let us have no cant of moderation," was its starting-point. " There is no public feeling in the country stronger than that of indignation against the Americans ; . . . conduct so base, so loathsome, so hateful. . . . As we urged the principle, No peace with Bonaparte ! so we must maintain the doctrine of, No peace with James Madison ! " [4] To this rule the " Times " steadily adhered with a degree of ill-temper not easily to be described, and with practical objects freely expressed. " Mr. Madison's dirty, swindling manœuvres in respect to Louisiana and the Floridas remain to be punished," it declared April 27 ; and May 17 it pursued the idea : " He must fall a victim to the just vengeance of the Federalists. Let us persevere. Let us unmask the impostor. . . . Who cares about the impudence

[1] The Times, Feb. 4 and 10, 1814.
[2] The Times, April 23, 1814.
[3] The Sun, Aug. 4, 1814.
[4] The Times, April 15, 1814.

which they call a doctrine? . . . We shall demand
indemnity. . . . We shall insist on security for Canada. . . . We shall inquire a little into the American
title to Louisiana; and we shall not permit the base
attack on Florida to go unpunished." May 18 it
declared that Madison had put himself on record as
a liar in the cause of his Corsican master. "He has
lived an impostor, and he deserves to meet the fate
of a traitor. That fate now stares him in the face."
May 24 the "Times" resumed the topic: "They are
struck to the heart with terror for their impending
punishment; and oh may no false liberality, no
mistaken lenity, no weak and cowardly policy, inter-
pose to save them from the blow! Strike! chastise
the savages, for such they are! . . . With Madison
and his perjured set no treaty can be made, for no
oath can bind them." When British commissioners
were at last announced as ready to depart for Ghent
to negotiate for peace with the United States, June 2,
the "Times" gave them instructions: "Our demands
may be couched in a single word, — Submission!"

The "Morning Post," a newspaper then carrying
higher authority than the "Times," used language
if possible more abusive, and even discovered, Jan.
18, 1814, "a new trait in the character of the
American government. Enjoying the reputation of
being the most unprincipled and the most contemptible on the face of the earth, they were already known
to be impervious to any noble sentiment; but it is
only of late that we find them insensible of the shame

of defeat, destitute even of the brutish quality of being beaten into a sense of their unworthiness and
their incapacity." Of Madison the " Morning Post"
held the lowest opinion. He was " a despot in disguise; a miniature imitation " and miserable tool of
Bonaparte, who wrote his Annual Message ; a sense-
less betrayer of his country.[1]

The " Times" and " Morning Post" were independent newspapers, and spoke only for themselves ;
but the " Courier" was supposed to draw inspiration
from the Government, and commonly received the
first knowledge of ministers' intentions. In temper
the " Courier" seemed obliged to vie with its less
favored rivals. The President's Annual Message of
1813 resembled in its opinion " all the productions of
that vain and vulgar Cabinet;" it was " a compound
of canting and hypocrisy, of exaggeration and falsehood, of coarseness without strength, of assertions
without proof, of the meanest prejudices, and of the
most malignant passions; of undisguised hatred of
Great Britain, and of ill-concealed partiality and ser-
vility toward France."[2] " We know of no man for
whom we feel greater contempt than for Mr. Madison," said the " Courier" of May 24. These illus-
trations of what the " Courier " called " exaggeration
and falsehood, of coarseness without strength, of assertions without proof, of the meanest prejudices,
and of the most malignant passions " were probably

[1] The Morning Post, Jan. 27 and Feb. 1, 1814.
[2] The Courier, Jan. 27, 1814.

in some degree a form as used by the " Courier,"
which would at a hint from the Ministry adopt a
different tone ; but announcements of official acts
and intentions were more serious, and claimed more
careful attention.

Immediately after the capitulation of Paris, March
31, the Ministry turned its attention to the United
States, and the " Courier " announced, April 15, that
twenty thousand men were to go from the Garonne
to America.   Mr. Madison, the " Courier " added,
had " made a pretty kettle of fish of it."   Twenty
thousand men were about two thirds of Wellington's
English force, and their arrival in America would,
as every Englishman believed, insure the success of
the campaign.   Not until these troops were embarked
would the Ministry begin to negotiate ; but in the
middle of May the military measures were complete,
and then the " Courier " began to prepare the public
mind for terms of peace.

These terms were the same as those announced by
the " Times," except that the " Courier " did not object to treating with Madison.   The United States
were to be interdicted the fisheries ; Spain was to be
supported in recovering Louisiana ; the right of impressment must be expressly conceded, — anything
short of this would be unwise and a disappointment.
" There are points which must be conceded by America before we can put an end to the contest." [1]   Such
language offered no apparent hope of peace; yet what-

[1] The Courier, May 19 and 24, 1814.

ever hope existed lay in Castlereagh, who inspired it. Extravagant as the demands were, they fell short of the common expectation. The " Courier " admitted the propriety of negotiation; it insisted neither on Madison's retirement nor on a division of the Union, and it refrained from asserting the whole British demand, or making it an ultimatum.

The chief pressure on the Ministry came from Canada, and could not be ignored. The Canadian government returned to its old complaint that Canadian interests had been ignorantly and wantonly sacrificed by the treaty of 1783, and that the opportunity to correct the wrong should not be lost. The Canadian official " Gazette " insisted that the United States should be required to surrender the northern part of the State of New York, and that both banks of the St. Lawrence should be Canadian property.[1] A line from Plattsburg to Sackett's Harbor would satisfy this necessity; but to secure Canadian interests, the British government should further insist on acquiring the east bank of tne Niagara River, and on a guaranty of the Indian Territory from Sandusky to Kaskaskias, with the withdrawal of American military posts in the Northwest. A pamphlet was published in May to explain the subject for the use of the British negotiators, and the required territorial cessions were marked on a map.[2] The control of

[1] Niles, vi. 322.

[2] Compressed view of the Points to be discussed in treating with America. London, 1814.

the Lakes, the Ohio River as the Indian boundary,
and the restitution of Louisiana were the chief sacri-
fices wished from the United States.   The cession
of a part of Maine was rather assumed than claimed,
and the fisheries were to be treated as wholly English.   A memorial from Newfoundland, dated Nov. 8,
1813,[1] pointed out the advantages which the war had
already brought to British trade and fisheries by
the exclusion of American competition, to the result
of doubling the number of men employed on the
Labrador shores ; and the memorialists added, —

"They cannot too often urge the important policy
. . . of wholly excluding foreigners from sharing again
in the advantages of a fishery from which a large proportion of our best national defence will be derived."

British confidence was at its highest point when
the Emperor of Russia and the King of Prussia
visited London, June 7, and received an enthusiastic
welcome.   Gallatin obtained an interview with the
Czar, June 17, and hoped that Russian influence
might moderate British demands ; but the Czar could
give him no encouragement.[2]   Gallatin wrote home
an often-quoted despatch, dated June 13, warning
the President that fifteen or twenty thousand men
were on their way to America, and that the United
States could expect no assistance from Europe.

"I have also the most perfect conviction," Gallatin
continued, "that under the existing unpropitious circumstances of the world, America cannot by a continuance

[1] Niles, vi. 238.   [2] Adams's Gallatin, p. 514.

of the war compel Great Britain to yield any of the maritime points in dispute, and particularly to agree to any satisfactory arrangement on the subject of impressment; and that the most favorable terms of peace that can be expected are the *status ante bellum*."

Even these terms, Gallatin added, depended on American success in withstanding the shock of the campaign. He did not say that at the time he wrote, the *status ante bellum* would be scouted by public opinion in England as favorable to the United States; but his estimate of the situation was more nearly exact than though he had consulted only the apparent passions of the British press.

"Lord Castlereagh," wrote Gallatin to Clay,[1] "is, according to the best information I can collect, the best disposed man in the Cabinet." Yet Castlereagh did not venture at that stage to show a disposition for peace. He delayed the negotiation, perhaps wisely, six weeks after the American negotiators had assembled at Ghent; and his instructions[2] to the British commissioners, dated July 28, reflected the demands of the press. They offered, not the *status ante bellum*, but the *uti possidetis*, as the starting-point of negotiation. "The state of possession must be considered as the territorial arrangement which would revive upon a peace, except so far as the same may be modified by any new treaty." The state of possession, in view of the orders that had then been

[1] Gallatin to Clay, April 22, 1814; Adams's Gallatin, p. 506.

[2] Castlereagh Correspondence, x. 67.

given, or were to be given, for the invasion of the
United States, was likely to cost the Americans half
of Maine, between the Penobscot and the Passamaquoddy; Plattsburg, and the northern part of New
York, Vermont, and New Hampshire; Fort Niagara,
Mackinaw, and possibly New Orleans and Mobile.
Besides this concession of the *uti possidetis*, or military occupation at the date of peace, the Americans
were required at the outset to admit as a *sine qua non*,
or condition precedent to any negotiation, that England's Indian allies, the tribes of the Northwestern
Territory, should be included in the pacification, and
that a definite boundary should be assigned to them
under a mutual guaranty of both Powers.   Eastport,
or Moose Island, and the fishing privileges were to
be regarded as British.   With these instructions of
July 28, the British commissioners, early in August,
started for Ghent.

Between Castlereagh's ideas and those of Madison
no relation existed.   Gallatin and his colleagues at
Ghent were provided with two sets of instructions.
The first set had been written in 1813, for the expected negotiation at Petersburg.   The second set
was written in January, 1814, and was brought to
Europe by Clay.   Neither authorized the American
commissioners to discuss such conditions as Castlereagh proposed.   The President gave his negotiators
authority to deal with questions of maritime law;
but even there they were allowed to exercise no discretion on the chief issue in dispute.   Monroe's latest

letter, dated January 28, was emphatic. "On impressment, as to the right of the United States to be ex-
empted from it, I have nothing to add," said the
secretary ; [1] " the sentiments of the President have
undergone no change on that important subject.
This degrading practice must cease ; our flag must
protect the crew, or the United States cannot consider themselves an independent nation." The President would consent to exclude all British seamen,
except those already naturalized, from American vessels, and to stipulate the surrender of British de-
serters ; but the express abandonment of impressment
was a *sine qua non* of treaty. " If this encroachment
of Great Britain is not provided against," said Monroe, " the United States have appealed to arms in
vain. If your efforts to accomplish it should fail,
all further negotiations will cease, and you will return
home without delay."

On territorial questions the two governments were
equally wide apart. So far from authorizing a cession of territorial rights, Monroe instructed the American commissioners, both at St. Petersburg and at
Ghent, " to bring to view the advantage to both
countries which is promised by a transfer of the
upper parts and even the whole of Canada to the
United States." [2] The instructions of January 1

[1] Instructions of Jan. 28, 1814; State Papers, Foreign Affairs,
iii. 701.
[2] Monroe's Instructions of June 23, 1813; MSS. State Department Records.

and January 28, 1814, reiterated the reasoning which should decide England voluntarily to cede Canada. "Experience has shown that Great Britain cannot participate in the dominion and navigation of the Lakes without incurring the danger of an early renewal of the war." [1]

These instructions were subsequently omitted from the published documents, probably because the Ghent commissioners decided not to act upon them; [2] but when the American negotiators met their British antagonists at Ghent, each party was under orders to exclude the other, if possible, from the Lakes, and the same divergence of opinion in regard to the results of two years' war extended over the whole field of negotiation. The British were ordered to begin by a *sine qua non* in regard to the Indians, which the Americans had no authority to consider. The Americans were ordered to impose a *sine qua non* in regard to impressments, which the British were forbidden to concede. The British were obliged to claim the basis of possession; the Americans were not even authorized to admit the status existing before the war. The Americans were required to negotiate about blockades, contraband and maritime rights of neutrals; the British could not admit such subjects into dispute. The British regarded their concessions of fishing-rights as terminated by

[1] Instructions of Jan. 1 and Jan. 28, 1814; MSS. State Department Records.

[2] Diary of J. Q. Adams, iii. 51.

the war; the Americans could not entertain the idea.

The diplomacy that should produce a treaty from such discordant material must show no ordinary excellence; yet even from that point of view the prospect was not encouraging. The British government made a peculiar choice of negotiators. The chief British commissioner, Lord Gambier, was unknown in diplomacy, or indeed in foreign affairs. A writer in the London "Morning Chronicle" of August 9 expressed the general surprise that Government could make no better selection for the chief of its commission than Lord Gambier, "who was a post-captain in 1794, and happened to fight the 'Defence' decently in Lord Howe's action; who slumbered for some time as a Junior Lord of the Admiralty; who sung psalms, said prayers, and assisted in the burning of Copenhagen, for which he was made a lord."

Gambier showed no greater fitness for his difficult task than was to be expected from his training; and the second member of the commission, Henry Goulburn, could not supply Gambier's deficiencies. Goulburn was Under-Secretary of State to Lord Bathurst; he was a very young man, but a typical under-secretary, combining some of Francis James Jackson's temper with the fixed opinions of the elder Rose, and he had as little idea of diplomacy as was to be expected from an Under-Secretary of State for the colonies. The third and last member was William Adams, Doctor of Civil Law, whose professional

knowledge was doubtless supposed to be valuable to
the commission, but who was an unknown man, and
remained one.

Experience had not convinced the British government that in dealing with the United States it required the best ability it could command.   The
mistake made by Lord Shelburne in 1783 was repeated by Lord Castlereagh in 1814.   The miscalcu-
lation of relative ability which led the Foreign Office
to assume that Gambier, Goulburn, and William
Adams were competent to deal with Gallatin, J. Q.
Adams, J. A. Bayard, Clay, and Russell was not reasonable.   Probably the whole British public service,
including Lords and Commons, could not at that day
have produced four men competent to meet Gallatin,
J. Q. Adams, Bayard, and Clay on the ground of
American interests ; and when Castlereagh opposed
to them Gambier, Goulburn, and Dr. Adams, he sacrificed whatever advantage diplomacy offered ; for in
diplomacy as in generalship, the individual commanded success.

The only serious difficulty in the American commission was its excess of strength.   By a natural
reaction against the attempt to abolish diplomatic
offices, the United States government sent into diplomacy its most vigorous men.   Under favorable
conditions, four minds and wills of so decided a
character could not easily work together ; but in the
Ghent commission an additional difficulty was created
by the unfortunate interference of the Senate.   Origi-

nally Gallatin, as was due to his age, services, and ability, had been the head of the St. Petersburg commission; but the Senate refused to confirm the appointment. The President at last removed Gallatin from the Treasury, and renominated him as a member of the Ghent commission after the other members had been nominated and confirmed. The Senate then gave its approval, — thus making Gallatin the last member of the commission instead of the first, and placing J. Q. Adams above them all.

Gallatin was peculiarly fitted to moderate a discordant body like the negotiators, while Adams was by temperament little suited to the post of moderator, and by circumstances ill-qualified to appear as a proper representative of the commission in the eyes of its other members. Unless Gallatin were one of the loftiest characters and most loyal natures ever seen in American politics, Adams's chance of success in controlling the board was not within reasonable hope. Gallatin was six years the senior, and represented the President, with the authority of close and continuous personal friendship. The board, including Adams himself, instinctively bowed to Gallatin's authority; but they were deferential to no one else, least of all to their nominal head. Bayard, whose age was the same as that of Adams, was still in name a Federalist; and although his party trusted him little more than it trusted Adams or William Pinkney, who had avowedly become Republicans, he was not the more disposed to follow Adams's leader-

ship. Clay, though ten years their junior, was the
most difficult of all to control; and Jonathan Russell, though a New Englander, preferred Clay's social
charm, and perhaps also his political prospects, to the
somewhat repellent temper and more than doubtful
popularity of Adams.

Personal rivalry and jealousies counted for much
in such a group; but these were not the only obstacles to Adams's influence. By a misfortune commonly reserved for men of the strongest wills, he
represented no one but himself and a powerless
minority. His State repudiated and, in a manner,
ostracized him. Massachusetts gave him no support,
even in defending her own rights; by every means
in her power she deprived him of influence, and
loaded him with the burden of her own unpopularity. Adams represented a community not only
hostile to the war, but avowedly laboring to produce
peace by means opposed to those employed at Ghent.
If the Ghent commission should succeed in making
a treaty, it could do so only by some sacrifice of
Massachusetts which would ruin Adams at home.
If the Ghent commission should fail, Adams must
be equally ruined by any peace produced through
the treasonable intrigues or overt rebellion of his
State.

Such a head to a commission so constituted needed
all the force of character which Adams had, and
some qualities he did not possess, in order to retain
enough influence to shape any project into a treaty

that he could consent to sign; while Gallatin's singular tact and nobility of character were never more likely to fail than in the effort to make allowance for the difficulties of his chief's position. Had Castlereagh improved the opportunity by sending to Ghent one competent diplomatist, or even a well-informed and intelligent man of business, like Alexander Baring, he might probably have succeeded in isolating Adams, and in negotiating with the other four commissioners a treaty sacrificing Massachusetts.

The five American commissioners were ready to negotiate in June; but Castlereagh, for obvious reasons, wished delay, and deferred action until August, doubtless intending to prevent the signature of a treaty on the basis of *uti possidetis* until after September, when Sherbrooke and Prevost should have occupied the territory intended to be held. In May and June no one in England, unless it were Cobbett, entertained more than a passing doubt of British success on land and water; least of all did the three British commissioners expect to yield British demands. They came to impose terms, or to break negotiation. They were not sent to yield any point in dispute, or to seek a cessation of arms.

At one o'clock on the afternoon of August 8, the first conference took place in the Hotel des Pays Bas at Ghent. After the usual civilities and forms had passed, Goulburn took the lead, and presented the points which he and his colleagues were authorized to discuss, — (1) Impressment and allegiance; (2)

the Indians and their boundary, a *sine qua non ;*
(3) the Canadian boundary; (4) the privilege of
landing and drying fish within British jurisdiction.
Goulburn declared that it was not intended to contest the right of the United States to the fisheries,
by which he probably meant the deep-sea fisheries ;
and he was understood to disavow the intention of
acquiring territory by the revision of the Canada
boundary ; but he urged an immediate answer upon
the question whether the Americans were instructed
on the point made a *sine qua non* by the British
government.

The Americans, seeing as yet only a small part
of the British demands, were not so much surprised
at Goulburn's points as unable to answer them.
The next day they replied in conference that they
had no authority to admit either Indian boundary or
fisheries into question, being without instructions on
these points ; and in their turn presented subjects
of discussion, — Blockades and Indemnities ; but
professed themselves willing to discuss everything.

In the conversation following this reply, the British
commissioners, with some apparent unwillingness,
avowed the intention of erecting the Indian Territory
into a barrier between the British possessions and the
United States; and the American commissioners declined even to retire for consultation on the possibility of agreeing to such an article.   The British
commissioners then proposed to suspend conferences
until they could receive further instructions, and their

wish was followed. Both parties sent despatches to their Governments.

Lord Castlereagh was prompt. As soon as was reasonably possible he sent more precise instructions. Dated August 14,[1] these supplementary instructions gave to those of July 28 a distinct outline. They proposed the Indian boundary fixed by the Treaty of Greenville for the permanent barrier between British and American dominion, beyond which neither government should acquire land. They claimed also a " rectification " of the Canadian frontier, and the cession of Fort Niagara and Sackett's Harbor, besides a permanent prohibition on the United States from keeping either naval forces or land fortifications on the Lakes. Beyond these demands the British commissioners were not for the present to go, nor were they to ask for a direct cession of territory for Canada " with any view to an acquisition of territory as such, but for the purpose of securing her possessions and preventing future disputes ; "[2] yet a small cession of land in Maine was necessary for a road from Halifax to Quebec, and an arrangement of the Northwestern boundary was required to coincide with the free navigation of the Mississippi.

As soon as the new instructions reached Ghent the British commissioners summoned the Americans to another conference, August 19 ; and Goulburn, read-

[1] Castlereagh Correspondence, x. 86.

[2] Note of British Commissioners, Aug. 19, 1814; State Papers, Foreign Affairs, iii. 710.

ing from Castlereagh's despatch, gave to the Americans a clear version of its contents.[1] When he had finished, Gallatin asked what was to be done with the American citizens — perhaps one hundred thousand in number — already settled beyond the Greenville line, in Ohio, Indiana, Illinois, and Michigan ? Goulburn and Dr. Adams replied that these people must shift for themselves. They added also that Moose Island and Eastport belonged to Great Britain as indisputably as the county of Northamptonshire, and were not a subject for discussion ; but they would not then make a *sine qua non* of the proposition regarding the Lakes. The conference ended, leaving the Americans convinced that their answer to these demands would close the negotiation. Clay alone, whose knowledge of the Western game of brag stood him in good stead, insisted that the British would recede.[2]

The British commissioners the next day, August 20, sent an official note containing their demands, and the Americans before sending their reply forwarded the note to America, with despatches dated August 19 and 20, announcing that they intended to return " a unanimous and decided negative." [3] They then undertook the task of drawing up their reply. Upon Adams as head of the commission fell

---

[1] Diary of J. Q. Adams, iii. 17, 18.

[2] Diary of J. Q. Adams, iii. 20, 101.

[3] Despatch of Aug. 19, 1814; State Papers, Foreign Affairs, iii. 708.

the duty of drafting formal papers, — a duty which, without common consent, no other member could assume. His draft met with little mercy, and the five gentlemen sat until eleven o'clock of August 24, "sifting, erasing, patching, and amending until we were all wearied, though none of us was yet satiated with amendment." At the moment when they gave final shape to the note which they believed would render peace impossible, the army of General Ross was setting fire to the Capitol at Washington, and President Madison was seeking safety in the Virginia woods.

Only to persons acquainted with the difficulties of its composition did the American note of August 24 show signs of its diverse origin.[1] In dignified temper, with reasoning creditable to its authors and decisive on its issues, it assured the British negotiators that any such arrangement as they required for the Indians was contrary to precedent in public law, was not founded on reciprocity, and was unnecessary for its professed object in regard to the Indians. The other demands were equally inadmissible : —

"They are founded neither on reciprocity, nor on any of the usual bases of negotiation, neither on that of *uti possidetis* nor of *status ante bellum*. They are above all dishonorable to the United States in demanding from them to abandon territory and a portion of their citizens ; to admit a foreign interference in their domestic concerns, and to cease to exercise their natural rights

[1] Note of Aug. 24, 1814 ; State Papers, Foreign Affairs, iii. 711.

on their own shores and in their own waters. A treaty
concluded on such terms would be but an armistice."

The negotiators were ready to terminate the war,
both parties restoring whatever territory might have
been taken, and reserving their rights over their re-
spective seamen ; but such demands as were made
by the British government could not be admitted even
for reference.

The American reply was sent to the British commissioners August 25, " and will bring the negotiation," remarked J. Q. Adams, " very shortly to a
close." [1] The American commissioners prepared to
quit Ghent and return to their several posts, while
the British commissioners waited for instructions
from London. Even Gallatin, who had clung to the
hope that he could effect an arrangement, abandoned
the idea, and believing that the British government
had adopted a system of conquest, prepared for an
immediate return to America. [2] Goulburn also noti-
fied his Government that the negotiation was not
likely to continue, and reported some confidential
warnings from Bayard that such conditions of peace
would not only insure war, but would sacrifice the
Federalist party. " It has not made the least impression upon me or upon my colleagues," reported
Goulburn to Bathurst. [3]

[1] Diary of J. Q. Adams, Aug. 25, 1814, iii. 23.

[2] Adams's Gallatin,. p. 524.

[3] Goulburn to Bathurst, Aug. 23, 1814; Wellington, Supplementary Despatches, ix. 189.

At that point the negotiation remained stationary for two months, kept alive by Liverpool, Castlereagh, and Bathurst, while they waited for the result of their American campaign. The despatch of August 20 crossed the Atlantic, and was communicated to Congress October 10, together with all other papers connected with the negotiation ; but not until October 25 did the American commissioners write again to their Government.

CHAPTER II.

THE British note of August 19 and the American rejoinder of August 24, brought about a situation where Lord Castlereagh's influence could make itself felt. Castlereagh had signed the British instructions of July 28 and August 14,[1] and himself brought the latter to Ghent, where he passed August 19, before going to Paris on his way to the Congress at Vienna. He was at Ghent when Goulburn and his colleagues held their conference and wrote their note of August 19;[2] and he could not be supposed ignorant of their language or acts. Yet when he received at Paris letters from Goulburn, dated August 24 and 26,[3] he expressed annoyance that the American commissioners should have been allowed to place England in the attitude of continuing the war for purposes of conquest, and still more that the British commissioners should be willing to accept that issue and break off negotiation upon it. In a letter

[1] Castlereagh Correspondence, x. 67, 86.

[2] Diary of J. Q. Adams, Aug. 19 and 20, 1814, iii. 19, 21.

[3] Goulburn to Bathurst, Aug. 24, 1814; Wellington Supplementary Despatches, ix. 190. Goulburn to Castlereagh, Aug. 26, 1814; Wellington Supplementary Despatches, ix. 193.

to Lord Bathurst, who took charge of the negotiation in his absence, Castlereagh suggested ideas altogether different from those till then advanced in England.[1]

"The substance of the question is," said Castlereagh, "Are we prepared to continue the war for territorial arrangements? And if not, is this the best time to make our peace, saving all our rights, and claiming the fisheries, which they do not appear to question? In which case the territorial questions might be reserved for ulterior discussion. Or is it desirable to take the chance of the campaign, and then to be governed by circumstances? . . . If we thought an immediate peace desirable, as they are ready to waive all the abstract questions, perhaps they might be prepared to sign a provisional article of Indian peace as distinct from limits, and relinquish their pretensions to the islands in Passamaquoddy Bay, and possibly to admit minor adjustments of frontier, including a right of communication from Quebec to Halifax across their territory. But while I state this, I feel the difficulty of so much letting down the question under present circumstances."

At the same time Castlereagh wrote to Goulburn, directing him to wait at Ghent for new instructions from London.[2] Lord Liverpool shared his disapproval of the manner in which the British commissioners had managed the case, and replied to Castlereagh,

[1] Castlereagh to Bathurst, Aug. 28. 1814: Castlereagh Correspondence, x. 100.

[2] Castlereagh to Goulburn, Aug. 28, 1814; Castlereagh Correspondence, x. 102.

September 2, that the Cabinet had already acted in
the sense he wished : [1] —

" Our commissioners had certainly taken a very erro-
neous view of our policy. If the negotiation had been allowed to break off upon the two notes already presented,
or upon such an answer as they were disposed to return,
I am satisfied that the war would have become quite
popular in America."

The idea that the war might become popular in
America was founded chiefly on the impossibility of
an Englishman's conceiving the contrary ; but in truth
the Ministry most feared that the war might become
unpopular in England.

" It is very material to throw the rupture of the negotiation, if it is to take place, upon the Americans," wrote
Liverpool, the same day, to the Duke of Wellington ; [2]
" and not to allow them to say that we have brought forward points as ultimata which were only brought forward
for discussion, and at the desire of the American commissioners themselves. The American note is a most im-
pudent one, and, as to all its reasoning, capable of an
irresistible answer."

New instructions were accordingly approved in Cabinet.[3] Drawn by Bathurst, and dated September 1,
they contained what Liverpool considered an " irresistible answer " to the American note of August 24 ;

[1] Liverpool to Castlereagh, Sept. 2, 1814 ; Wellington Supplementary Despatches, ix. 214.

[2] Liverpool to Wellington, Sept. 2, 1814; Wellington Supplementary Despatches, ix. 212.

[3] Draft of note, etc., Sept. 1, 1814 ; Wellington Supplementary Despatches, ix. 245.

but their force of logic was weakened by the admission that the previous British demands, though certainly stated as a *sine qua non*, were in reality not to be regarded as such. In private this retreat was covered by the pretext that it was intended only to keep the negotiation alive until better terms could be exacted.

"We cannot expect that the negotiation will proceed at present," continued Liverpool's letter to Castlereagh; "but I think it not unlikely, after our note has been delivered in, that the American commissioners will propose to refer the subject to their Government. In that case the negotiation may be adjourned till the answer is received, and we shall know the result of the campaign before it can be resumed. If our commander does his duty, I am persuaded we shall have acquired by our arms every point on the Canadian frontier which we ought to insist on keeping."

Lord Gambier and his colleagues communicated their new instructions to the American negotiators in a long note dated September 4, and were answered by a still longer note dated September 9, which was also sent to London, and considered in Cabinet. Bathurst felt no anxiety about the negotiation in its actual stage. Goulburn wrote to him that "as long as we answer their notes, I believe that they will be ready to give us replies," and urged only that Sir George Prevost should hasten his reluctant movements in Canada.[1]

[1] Goulburn to Bathurst, Sept. 5 and 16, 1814 ; Wellington Supplementary Despatches, ix. 221, 265.

Bathurst wrote more instructions, dated September 16, directing his commissioners to abandon the demands for Indian territory and exclusive control of the Lakes, and to ask only that the Indians should be included in the peace.[1] The British commissioners sent their note with these concessions to the Americans September 19; and then for the first time the Americans began to suspect the possibility of serious negotiation. For six weeks they had dealt only with the question whether they should negotiate at all.

The demand that the Indians should be included in the treaty was one that under favorable circumstances the Americans would have rejected; but none of them seriously thought of rejecting it as their affairs then stood. When the American commissioners discussed the subject among themselves, September 20, Adams proposed to break off the negotiation on that issue; but Gallatin good-naturedly overruled him, and Adams would not himself, on cool reflection, have ventured to take such responsibility. Indeed, he suggested an article for an Indian amnesty, practically accepting the British demand.[2] He also yielded to Gallatin the ungrateful task of drafting the answers to the British notes; and thus Gallatin became in effect the head of the commission.

All Gallatin's abilities were needed to fill the place. In his entire public life he had never been required to

[1] Draft of note, etc., Sept. 16, 1814; Wellington Supplementary Despatches, ix. 263.

[2] Diary of J. Q. Adams, Sept. 20, 1814, iii. 38.

manage so unruly a set of men. The British commissioners were trying, and especially Goulburn was aggressive in temper and domineering in tone; but with them Gallatin had little trouble. Adams and Clay were persons of a different type, as far removed from British heaviness as they were from the Virginian ease of temper which marked the Cabinet of Jefferson, or the incompetence which characterized that of Madison. Gallatin was obliged to exert all his faculties to control his colleagues; but whenever he succeeded, he enjoyed the satisfaction of feeling that he had colleagues worth controlling. They were bent on combat, if not with the British, at all events with each other; and Gallatin was partly amused and partly annoyed by the unnecessary energy of their attitude.

The first divergence occurred in framing the reply to the British note of September 19, which while yielding essentials made a series of complaints against the United States, — and among the rest reproached them for their attempt to conquer Canada, and their actual seizure of Florida. Adams, who knew little about the secrets of Jefferson's and Madison's Administrations, insisted on resenting the British charges, and especially on justifying the United States government in its attacks upon Florida. Bayard protested that he could not support such a view, because he had himself publicly in Congress denounced the Government on the subject of Florida; and Gallatin was almost equally committed, for, as he frankly said, he had opposed in Cabinet for a whole year what had been done in Florida before he could succeed in stopping it.[1] Clay said nothing, but he had strong reasons for wishing that the British negotiators should not be challenged to quote his notorious speeches on the conquest of Canada. Adams produced Monroe's instructions, and in the end compelled his colleagues to yield. His mistake in pressing such an issue was obvious to every one but himself, and would have been evident to him had he not been blinded by irritation at the British note. His colleagues retaliated by summarily rejecting as cant his argument that moral and religious duty required the Americans to take and settle the land of the Indians.[2]

After much discussion their note was completed and sent, September 26, to the British commissioners,[3] who forwarded it as usual to London, with a letter from Goulburn of the same date, written in the worst possible temper, and charging the American commissioners with making a variety of false and fraudulent statements.[4] While the British Cabinet detained it longer than usual for consideration, the Americans at Ghent felt their position grow weaker day by day.

[1] Diary of J. Q. Adams, Sept. 25, 1814, iii. 41.

[2] Diary of J. Q. Adams, Sept. 25, 1814, iii. 42.

[3] American note of Sept. 26, 1814; State Papers, Foreign Affairs, iii. 719.

[4] Goulburn to Bathurst, Sept. 26, 1814; Wellington Supplementary Despatches, ix. 287.

Nothing warranted a serious hope of peace. Goulburn and his colleagues showed no thought of yielding acceptable conditions. The London "Courier" of September 29 announced what might be taken for a semi-official expression of the Ministry : —

"Peace they [the Americans] may make, but it must be on condition that America has not a foot of land on the waters of the St. Lawrence, . . . no settlement on the Lakes, . . . no renewal of the treaties of 1783 and 1794 ; . . . and they must explicitly abandon their new-fangled principles of the law of nations."

Liverpool, writing to Castlereagh September 23,[1] said that in his opinion the Cabinet had "now gone to the utmost justifiable point in concession, and if they [the Americans] are so unreasonable as to reject our proposals, we have nothing to do but to fight it out. The military accounts from America are on the whole satisfactory." The news of the cruel humiliation at Bladensburg and the burning of Washington arrived at Ghent October 1, and caused British and Americans alike to expect a long series of British triumphs, especially on Lake Champlain, where they knew the British force to be overwhelming.

Goulburn exerted himself to produce a rupture. His letter of September 26 to Bathurst treated the American offer of an Indian amnesty as a rejection of the British ultimatum. Again Lord Bathurst set him right by sending him, October 5, the draft of a recip-

[1] Liverpool to Castlereagh, Sept. 23, 1814 ; Wellington Supplementary Despatches, ix. 278.

rocal article replacing the Indians in their situation
before the war: and the British commissioners in a
note dated October 8, 1814, communicated this article
once more as an ultimatum.[1] Harrison's treaty of
July 22 with the Wyandots, Delawares, Shawanees,
and other tribes, binding them to take up arms
against the British, had then arrived, and this news
lessened the interest of both parties in the Indian
question. None of the American negotiators were
prepared to break off negotiations on that point at
such a time, and Clay was so earnest to settle the
matter that he took from Gallatin and Adams the
task of writing the necessary acceptance of the British ultimatum. Gallatin and Clay decided to receive
the British article as according entirely with the American offer of amnesty, and the note was so written.[2]

With this cordial admission of the British ultimatum the Americans coupled an intimation that the
time had come when an exchange of general projects
for the proposed treaty should be made. More than
two months of discussion had then resulted only in
eliminating the Indians from the dispute, and in
agreeing to maintain silence in regard to the Lakes.
Another great difficulty which had been insuperable
was voluntarily removed by President Madison and his
Cabinet, who after long and obstinate resistance at

[1] British note of Oct. 8, 1814; State Papers, Foreign Affairs,
iii. 721.

[2] American note of Oct. 13, 1814; State Papers, Foreign Affairs, iii. 723.

last authorized the commissioners, by instructions
dated June 27, to omit impressment from the treaty.
Considering the frequent positive declarations of
the United States government, besides the rejection
of Monroe's treaty in 1807 and of Admiral Warren's and Sir George Prevost's armistice of 1812 for
want of an explicit concession on that point, Monroe's letter of June 27 was only to be excused as an
act of common-sense or of necessity. The President
preferred to represent it as an act of common-sense,
warranted by the peace in Europe, which promised to
offer no further occasion for the claim or the denial
of the British right. On the same principle the subject of blockades was withdrawn from discussion; and
these concessions, balanced by the British withdrawal
from the Indian ultimatum and the Lake armaments,
relieved the American commissioners of all their insuperable difficulties.

The British commissioners were not so easily res-
cued from their untenable positions. The American
note of October 13, sent as usual to London, was
answered by Bathurst October 18 and 20,[1] in instructions revealing the true British terms more
completely than had yet been ventured. Bathurst
at length came to the cardinal point of the negotiation. As the American commissioners had said
in their note of August 24, the British government
must choose between the two ordinary bases of treaties of peace, — the state before the war, or *status*

[1] Castlereagh Correspondence, x. 168–173.

ante bellum ; and the state of possession, or *uti pos-sidetis.* Until the middle of October, 1814, the *uti possidetis*, as a basis of negotiation, included whatever country might have been occupied by Sir George Prevost in his September campaign. Bathurst from the first intended to insist on the state of possession, but had not thought proper to avow it. His instructions of October 18 and 20 directed the British commissioners to come to the point, and to claim the basis of *uti possidetis* from the American negotiators : —

" On their admitting this to be the basis on which they are ready to negotiate, but not before they have admitted it, you will proceed to state the mutual accommodations which may be entered into in conformity with this basis. The British occupy Fort Michillimackinaw, Fort Niagara, and all the country east of the Penobscot. On the other hand the forces of the United States occupy Fort Erie and Fort Amherstburg [Malden]. On the government of the United States consenting to restore these two forts, Great Britain is ready to restore the forts of Castine and Machias, retaining Fort Niagara and Fort Michillimackinaw."

Thus the British demand, which had till then been intended to include half of Maine and the whole south bank of the St. Lawrence River from Plattsburg to Sackett's Harbor, suddenly fell to a demand for Moose Island, a right of way across the northern angle of Maine, Fort Niagara with five miles circuit, and the Island of Mackinaw. The reason for the new spirit of moderation was not far to seek. On the afternoon of October 17, while the British Cabinet was still deliberating on the basis of *uti possidetis*, news reached London that the British invasion of northern New York, from which so much had been expected, had totally failed, and that Prevost's large army had precipitately retreated into Canada. The London "Times" of October 19 was frank in its expressions of disappointment : —

" This is a lamentable event to the civilized world. . . . The subversion of that system of fraud and malignity which constitutes the whole policy of the Jeffersonian school . . . was an event to which we should have bent and yet must bend all our energies. The present American government must be displaced, or it will sooner or later plant its poisoned dagger in the heart of the parent State."

The failure of the attempt on Baltimore and Drummond's bloody repulse at Fort Erie became known at the same time, and coming together at a critical moment threw confusion into the Ministry and their agents in the press and the diplomatic service throughout Europe. The " Courier " of October 25 declared that " peace with America is neither practicable nor desirable till we have wiped away this late disaster ; " but the " Morning Chronicle" of October 21–24 openly intimated that the game of war was at an end. October 31, the Paris correspondent of the London " Times " told of the cheers that rose from the crowds in the Palais Royal gardens at each

recital of the Plattsburg defeat; and October 21
Goulburn wrote from Ghent to Bathurst,[1] —

" The news from America is very far from satisfactory.
Even our brilliant success at Baltimore, as it did not terminate in the capture of the town, will be considered by
the Americans as a victory and not as an escape. . . .
If it were not for the want of fuel in Boston, I should be
quite in despair."

In truth the blockade was the single advantage
held by England; and even in that advantage the
Americans had a share as long as their cruisers surrounded the British Islands.

Liverpool wrote to Castlereagh, October 21,[2] commenting severely on Prevost's failure, and finding
consolation only in the thought that the Americans
showed themselves even less patriotic than he had
supposed them to be : —

" The capture and destruction of Washington has not
united the Americans : quite the contrary. We have
gained more credit with them by saving private property
than we have lost by the destruction of their public
works and buildings. Madison clings to office, and I
am strongly inclined to think that the best thing for us
is that he should remain there."

Castlereagh at Vienna found himself unable to
make the full influence of England felt, so long as

[1] Goulburn to Bathurst ; Wellington Supplementary Despatches, ix. 366.

[2] Liverpool to Castlereagh, Oct. 21, 1814 ; Wellington Supplementary Despatches, ix. 367.

such mortifying disasters by land and sea proved
her inability to deal with an enemy she persisted in
calling contemptible.

On the American commissioners the news came,
October 21, with the effect of a reprieve from execution. Gallatin was deeply moved; Adams could not
believe the magnitude of the success; but as far as
regarded their joint action, the overthrow of England's scheme produced no change. Their tone had
always been high, and they saw no advantage to be
gained by altering it. The British commissioners
sent to them, October 21, the substance of the new
instructions, offering the basis of *uti possidetis*, subject to modifications for mutual convenience.[1] The
Americans by common consent, October 23, declined
to treat on that basis, or on any other than the
mutual restoration of territory.[2] They thought that
the British government was still playing with them,
when in truth Lord Bathurst had yielded the chief
part of the original British demand, and had come
to what the whole British empire regarded as essentials, — the right of way to Quebec, and the exclusion of American fishermen from British shores
and waters.

The American note of October 24, bluntly rejecting
the basis of *uti possidetis*, created a feeling akin to

[1] British note of Oct. 21, 1814; State Papers, Foreign Affairs,
iii. 724.

[2] American note of Oct. 24, 1814; State Papers, Foreign
Affairs, iii. 725.

consternation in the British Cabinet. At first, ministers assumed that the war must go on, and deliberated only on the point to be preferred for a rupture. "We still think it desirable to gain a little more time before the negotiation is brought to a close," wrote Liverpool to the Duke of Wellington,[1] October 28; and on the same day he wrote to Castlereagh at Vienna to warn him that the American war "will probably now be of some duration," and treating of its embarrassments without disguise.[2] The Czar's conduct at Vienna had annoyed and alarmed all the great Powers, and the American war gave him a decisive advantage over England ; but even without the Russian complication, the prospect for ministers was not cheering.

"Looking to a continuance of the American war, our financial state is far from satisfactory," wrote Lord Liverpool; " . . . the American war will not cost us less than £10,000,000, in addition to our peace establishment and other expenses. We must expect, therefore, to hear it said that the property tax is continued for the purpose of securing a better frontier for Canada."

A week passed without bringing encouragement to the British Cabinet. On the contrary the Ministry learned that a vigorous prosecution of hostilities would cost much more than ten million pounds, and

[1] Liverpool to Wellington, Oct. 28, 1814; Wellington Supplementary Despatches, ix. 384.

[2] Liverpool to Castlereagh, Oct. 28, 1814 ; Wellington Supplementary Despatches, ix. 382.

when Liverpool next wrote to Castlereagh, November 2,[1] although he could still see " little prospect for our negotiations at Ghent ending in peace," he added that " the continuance of the American war will entail upon us a prodigious expense, much more than we had any idea of." A Cabinet meeting was to be held the next day, November 3, to review the whole course of policy as to America.

Throughout the American difficulties, from first to last, the most striking quality shown by the British government was the want of intelligence which caused the war, and marked the conduct of both the war and the negotiations. If the foreign relations of every government were marked by the same character, politics could be no more than rivalry in the race to blunder; but in October, 1814, another quality almost equally striking became evident. The weakness of British councils was as remarkable as their want of intelligence. The government of England had exasperated the Americans to an animosity that could not forget or forgive, and every dictate of self-interest required that it should carry out its policy to the end. Even domestic politics in Parliament might have been more easily managed by drawing public criticism to America, while in no event could taxes be reduced to satisfy the public demand.[2] Another year

---

[1] Liverpool to Castlereagh, Nov. 2, 1814; Wellington Supplementary Despatches, ix. 382.

[2] Liverpool to Castlereagh, Jan. 16, 1815; Castlereagh Correspondence, x. 240.

of war was the consistent and natural course for ministers to prefer.

So the Cabinet evidently thought; but instead of making a decision, the Cabinet council of November 3 resorted to the expedient of shifting responsibility upon the Duke of Wellington. The Duke was then Ambassador at Paris. His life had been threatened by angry officers of Napoleon, who could not forgive his victories at Vittoria and Toulouse. For his own security he might be sent to Canada, and if he went, he should go with full powers to close the war as he pleased.

The next day, November 4, Liverpool wrote to Wellington, explaining the wishes of the Cabinet, and inviting him to take the entire command in Canada, in order to bring the war to an honorable conclusion.[1] Wellington replied November 9, — and his words were the more interesting because, after inviting and receiving so decided an opinion from so high an authority, the Government could not easily reject it. Wellington began by reviewing the military situation, and closed by expressing his opinion on the diplomatic contest:[2] —

"I have already told you and Lord Bathurst that I feel no objection to going to America, though I don't

[1] Liverpool to Wellington, Nov. 4, 1814; Liverpool to Castlereagh, Nov. 4, 1814; Wellington Supplementary Despatches, ix. 404, 405.

[2] Wellington to Castlereagh, Nov. 9, 1814; Wellington Supplementary Despatches, i. 426.

promise to myself much success there. I believe there
are troops enough there for the defence of Canada forever, and even for the accomplishment of any reasonable
offensive plan that could be formed from the Canadian
frontier. I am quite sure that all the American armies
of which I have ever read would not beat out of a field
of battle the troops that went from Bordeaux last summer, if common precautions and care were taken of
them. That which appears to me to be wanting in
America is not a general, or a general officer and troops,
but a naval superiority on the Lakes."

These views did not altogether accord with those
of Americans, who could not see that the British
generals made use of the Lakes even when controlling
them, but who saw the troops of Wellington retire
from one field of battle after another, — at Plattsburg,
Baltimore, and New Orleans, — while taking more
than common precautions   Wellington's military
comments showed little interest in American affairs,
and evidently he saw nothing to be gained by going
to Canada. His diplomatic ideas betrayed the same
bias : —

"In regard to your present negotiations, I confess that
I think you have no right, from the state of the war, to
demand any concession of territory from America. . . .
You have not been able to carry it into the enemy's territory, notwithstanding your military success and now un-
doubted military superiority, and have not even cleared
your own territory on the point of attack. You cannot
on any principle of equality in negotiation claim a cession of territory excepting in exchange for other advan-

tages which you have in your power. . . . Then if this reasoning be true, why stipulate for the *uti possidetis?* You can get no territory ; indeed, the state of your military operations, however creditable, does not entitle you to demand any."

After such an opinion from the first military authority of England, the British Ministry had no choice but to abandon its claim for territory. Wellington's letter reached London about November 13, and was duly considered in the Cabinet. Liverpool wrote to Castlereagh, November 18, that the Ministry had made its decision ; the claim for territory was to be abandoned. For this retreat he alleged various excuses, — such as the unsatisfactory state of the negotiations at Vienna, and the alarming condition of France ; the finances, the depression of rents, and the temper of Parliament.[1] Such reasoning would have counted for nothing in the previous month of May, but six months wrought a change in public feeling. The war had lost public favor. Even the colonial and shipping interests and the navy were weary of it, while the army had little to expect from it but hard service and no increase of credit. Every Englishman who came in contact with Americans seemed to suffer. Broke, the only victor by sea, was a lifelong invalid ; and Brock and Ross, the only victors on land, had paid for their success with their lives. Incessant disappointment made the war an unpleasant

[1] Liverpool to Castlereagh, Nov. 18, 1814; Wellington Supplementary Despatches, ix. 438.

thought with Englishmen. The burning of Washington was an exploit of which they could not boast. The rate of marine insurance was a daily and intolerable annoyance So rapidly did the war decline in favor, that in the first half of December it was declared to be decidedly unpopular by one of the most judicious English liberals, Francis Horner; although Horner held that the Americans, as the dispute then stood, were the aggressors.[1] The tone of the press showed the same popular tendency, for while the "Times" grumbled loudly over the Canada campaign, the "Morning Chronicle" no longer concealed its hostility to the war, and ventured to sneer at it, talking of "the entire defeat and destruction of the last British fleet but one; for it has become necessary to particularize them now."[2]

While the Cabinet still waited, the first instalment of Ghent correspondence to August 20, published in America October 10, returned to England November 18, and received no flattering attention. "We cannot compliment our negotiators," remarked the "Morning Chronicle;" and the "Times" was still less pleased. "The British government has been tricked into bringing forward demands which it had not the power to enforce. . . . Why treat at all with Mr. Madison?" In Parliament, November 19, the liberal opposition attacked the Government

[1] Horner to J. A. Murray, Dec. 10, 1814; Horner's Memoirs, ii. 213.

[2] The Morning Chronicle, Nov. 19, 1814. .

for setting up novel pretensions. Ministers needed no more urging, and Bathurst thenceforward could not be charged with waste of time.

During this interval of more than three weeks the negotiators at Ghent were left to follow their own devices. In order to provide the Americans with occupation, the British commissioners sent them a note dated October 31 calling for a counter-project, since the basis of *uti possidetis* was refused.[1] This note, with all the others since August 20, was sent by the Americans to Washington on the same day, October 31 ; and then Gallatin and Adams began the task of drafting the formal project of a treaty. Immediately the internal discords of the commission broke into earnest dispute. A struggle began between the East and the West over the fisheries and the Mississippi.

The treaty of 1783 coupled the American right of fishing in British waters and curing fish on British shores with the British right of navigating the Mississippi River. For that arrangement the elder Adams was responsible. The fisheries were a Massachusetts interest. At Paris in 1783 John Adams, in season and out of season, with his colleagues and with the British negotiators, insisted, with the intensity of conviction, that the fishing rights which the New England people held while subjects of the British crown were theirs by no grant or treaty, but as

[1] British note of Oct. 31, 1814; State Papers, Foreign Relations, iii. 726.

a natural right, which could not be extinguished by war; and that where British subjects had a right to fish, whether on coasts or shores, in bays, inlets, creeks, or harbors, Americans had the same right, to be exercised wherever and whenever they pleased. John Adams's persistence secured the article of the definitive treaty, which, without expressly admitting a natural right, coupled the in-shore fisheries and the navigation of the Mississippi with the recognition of independence. In 1814 as in 1783 John Adams clung to his trophies, and his son would have waged indefinite war rather than break his father's heart by sacrificing what he had won; but at Ghent the son stood in isolation which the father in the worst times had never known. Massachusetts left him to struggle alone for a principle that needed not only argument but force to make it victorious. Governor Strong did not even write to him as he did to Pickering, that Massachusetts would give an equivalent in territory for the fisheries. As far as the State could influence the result, the fisheries were to be lost by default.

Had Adams encountered only British opposition he might have overborne it as his father had done; but since 1783 the West had become a political power, and Louisiana had been brought into the Union. If the fisheries were recognized as an indefeasible right by the treaty of 1783, the British liberty of navigating the Mississippi was another indefeasible right, which must revive with peace. The Western people

naturally objected to such a proposition. Neither
they nor the Canadians could be blamed for unwillingness to impose a mischievous servitude forever
upon their shores, and Clay believed his popularity
to depend on preventing an express recognition of
the British right to navigate the Mississippi. Either
Clay or Adams was sure to refuse signing any
treaty which expressly sacrificed the local interests
of either.

In this delicate situation only the authority and
skill of Gallatin saved the treaty. At the outset of
the discussion, October 30, Gallatin quietly took the
lead from Adams's hands, and assumed the champion-
ship of the fisheries by proposing to renew both privileges, making the one an equivalent for the other.
Clay resisted obstinately, while Gallatin gently and
patiently overbore him. When Gallatin's proposal
was put to the vote November 5, Clay and Russell
alone opposed it, — and the support then given by
Russell to Clay was never forgotten by Adams. Clay
still refusing to sign the offer, Gallatin continued his
pressure, until at last, November 10, Clay consented
to insert, not in the project of treaty, but in the
note which accompanied it, a paragraph declaring
that the commissioners were not authorized to bring
into discussion any of the rights hitherto enjoyed
in the fisheries: " From their nature, and from the
peculiar character of the treaty of 1783 by which
they were recognized, no further stipulation has been
deemed necessary by the Government of the United

States to entitle them to the full enjoyment of all of them."

Clay signed the note,[1] though unwillingly; and it was sent, November 10, with the treaty project, to the British commissioners, who forwarded it to London, where it arrived at the time when the British Cabinet had at last decided on peace. Bathurst sent his reply in due course; and Goulburn's disgust was great to find that instead of breaking negotiation on the point of the fisheries as he wished,[2] he was required once more to give way. "You know that I was never much inclined to give way to the Americans," he wrote, November 25.[3] "I am still less inclined to do so after the statement of our demands with which the negotiation opened, and which has in every point of view proved most unfortunate."

The British reply, dated November 26,[4] took no notice of the American reservation as to the fisheries, but inserted in the project the old right of navigating the Mississippi. Both Bathurst and Goulburn thought that their silence, after the American declaration, practically conceded the American right to the fisheries, though Gambier and Dr. Adams thought

[1] American note of Nov. 10, 1814; State Papers, Foreign Relations, iii. 733.

[2] Goulburn to Bathurst, Nov. 10, 1814; Wellington Supplementary Despatches, ix. 427.

[3] Goulburn to Bathurst, Nov. 10, 1814; Wellington Supplementary Despatches, ix. 452.

[4] British note of Nov. 26, 1814; State Papers, Foreign Relations, iii. 740.

differently.[1] In either case the British note of November 26, though satisfactory to Adams, was far
from agreeable to Clay, who was obliged to endanger
the peace in order to save the Mississippi. Adams
strongly inclined to take the British project precisely as it was offered,[2] but Gallatin overruled him,
and Clay would certainly have refused to sign. In
discussing the subject, November 28, Gallatin proposed to accept the article on the navigation of the
Mississippi if the British would add a provision recog-
nizing the fishing rights. Clay lost his temper, and
intimated something more than willingness to let
Massachusetts pay for the pleasure of peace;[3] but
during the whole day of November 28, and with the
same patience November 29, Gallatin continued urging Clay and restraining Adams, until at last on the
third day he brought the matter to the point he
wished.

The result of this long struggle saved not indeed
the fisheries, but the peace. Clay made no further
protest when, in conference with the British commissioners December 1, the Americans offered to renew
both the disputed rights.[4] Their proposal was sent to
London, and was answered by Bathurst December 6,
in a letter offering to set aside for future negotiation

[1] Goulburn to Bathurst, Nov. 25, 1814 ; Wellington Supplementary Despatches, ix. 452.

[2] Diary of J. Q. Adams, Nov. 27, 1814, iii. 70.

[3] Diary of J. Q. Adams, iii. 72.

[4] Protocol of Dec. 1, 1814 ; State Papers, Foreign Relations,
iii. 742.

the terms under which the old fishing liberty and the navigation of the Mississippi should be continued for fair equivalents.[1] The British commissioners communicated this suggestion in conference December 10, and threw new dissension among the Americans.

The British offer to reserve both disputed rights for future negotiation implied that both rights were forfeited, or subject to forfeit, by war, — an admission which Adams could not make, but which the other commissioners could not reject. At that point Adams found himself alone. Even Gallatin admitted that the claim to the natural right of catching and curing fish on British shores was untenable, and could never be supported. Adams's difficulties were the greater because the question of peace and war was reduced to two points, — the fisheries and Moose Island, — both interesting to Massachusetts alone. Yet the Americans were unwilling to yield without another struggle, and decided still to resist the British claim as inconsistent with the admitted basis of the *status ante bellum*.

The struggle with the British commissioners then became warm. A long conference, December 12, brought no conclusion. The treaty of 1783 could neither be followed nor ignored, and perplexed the Englishmen as much as the Americans. During December 13 and December 14, Adams continued to

[1] Bathurst to the Commissioners, Dec. 6, 1814; Castlereagh Correspondence, x. 214.

press his colleagues to assert the natural right to the fisheries, and to insist on the permanent character of the treaty of 1783 ; but Gallatin would not consent to make that point an ultimatum. All the commissioners except Adams resigned themselves to the sacrifice of the fisheries ; but Gallatin decided to make one more effort before abandoning the struggle, and with that object drew up a note rejecting the British stipulation because it implied the abandonment of a right, but offering either to be silent as to both the fisheries and the Mississippi, or to admit a general reference to further negotiation of all subjects in dispute, so expressed as to imply no abandonment of right.

The note was signed and sent December 14,[1] and the Americans waited another week for the answer. Successful as they had been in driving their British antagonists from one position after another, they were not satisfied. Adams still feared that he might not be able to sign, and Clay was little better pleased. " He said we should make a damned bad treaty, and he did not know whether he would sign it or not."[2] Whatever Adams thought of the treaty, his respect for at least two of his colleagues was expressed in terms of praise rarely used by him. Writing to his wife, September 27,[3] Adams said : " Mr. Gallatin

[1] American note of Dec. 14, 1814; State Papers, Foreign Relations, iii. 743.

[2] Diary of J. Q. Adams, Dec. 14, 1814, iii. 118.

[3] J. Q. Adams to his wife, Sept. 27, 1814 ; Adams MSS.

keeps and increases his influence over us all. It would have been an irreparable loss if our country had been deprived of the benefit of his talents in this negotiation." At the moment of final suspense he wrote again, December 16 : —

"Of the five members of the American mission, the Chevalier [Bayard] has the most perfect control of his temper, the most deliberate coolness ; and it is the more meritorious because it is real self-command. His feelings are as quick and his spirits as high as those of any one among us, but he certainly has them more under government. I can scarcely express to you how much both he and Mr. Gallatin have risen in my esteem since we have been here living together. Gallatin has not quite so constant a supremacy over his own emotions ; yet he seldom yields to an ebullition of temper, and recovers from it immediately. He has a faculty, when discussion grows too warm, of turning off its edge by a joke, which I envy him more than all his other talents ; and he has in his character one of the most extraordinary combinations of stubbornness and of flexibility that I ever met with in man. His greatest fault I think to be an ingenuity sometimes trenching upon ingenuousness."

Gallatin's opinion of Adams was not so enthusiastic as Adams's admiration for him. He thought Adams's chief fault to be that he lacked judgment " to a deplorable degree." [1] Of Clay, whether in his merits or his faults, only one opinion was possible. Clay's character belonged to the simple Southern or Virginia type, somewhat affected, but

[1] Adams's Gallatin, p. 599.

not rendered more complex, by Western influence, — and transparent beyond need of description or criticism.

The extraordinary patience and judgment of Gallatin, aided by the steady support of Bayard, carried all the American points without sacrificing either Adams or Clay, and with no quarrel of serious importance on any side. When Lord Bathurst received the American note of December 14, he replied December 19, yielding the last advantage he possessed:[1] " The Prince Regent regrets to find that there does not appear any prospect of being able to arrive at such an arrangement with regard to the fisheries as would have the effect of coming to a full and satisfactory explanation on that subject;" but since this was the case, the disputed article might be altogether omitted.

Thus the treaty became simply a cessation of hostilities, leaving every claim on either side open for future settlement. The formality of signature was completed December 24, and closed an era of American history. In substance, the treaty sacrificed much on both sides for peace. The Americans lost their claims for British spoliations, and were obliged to admit question of their right to Eastport and their fisheries in British waters ; the British failed to establish their principles of impressment and blockade, and admitted question of their right to navigate the Mississippi and trade with the Indians.

[1] Castlereagh Correspondence, x. 221.

Perhaps at the moment the Americans were the chief losers; but they gained their greatest triumph in referring all their disputes to be settled by time, the final negotiator, whose decision they could safely trust.

CHAPTER III.

ENGLAND received the Treaty of Ghent with feelings of mixed anger and satisfaction. The "Morning Chronicle" seemed surprised at the extreme interest which the news excited. As early as November 24, when ministers made their decision to concede the American terms, the "Morning Chronicle" announced that "a most extraordinary sensation was produced yesterday" by news from Ghent, and by reports that ministers had abandoned their ground. When the treaty arrived, December 26, the same Whig newspaper, the next morning, while asserting that ministers had "humbled themselves in the dust and thereby brought discredit on the country," heartily approved what they had done; and added that "the city was in a complete state of hurricane during the whole of yesterday, but the storm did not attain its utmost height until toward the evening. . . . Purchases were made to the extent of many hundred thousand pounds." The importance of the United States to England was made more apparent by the act of peace than by the pressure of war. "At Birmingham," said the "Courier," "an immense assemblage witnessed the arrival of the mail, and immediately took the horses out, and drew the mail to the post-office with the loudest acclamations," — acclamations over a treaty universally regarded as discreditable.

The " Times " admitted the general joy, and denied only that it was universal. If the " Times " in any degree represented public opinion, the popular satisfaction at the peace was an extraordinary political symptom, for in its opinion the Government had accepted terms such as " might have been expected from an indulgent and liberal conqueror. . . . We have retired from the combat," it said, December 30, " with the stripes yet bleeding on our back, — with the recent defeats at Plattsburg and on Lake Champlain unavenged." During several succeeding weeks the " Times " continued its extravagant complaints, which served only to give the Americans a new idea of the triumph they had won.

In truth, no one familiar with English opinion during the past ten years attempted to deny that the government of England must admit one or the other of two conclusions, — either it had ruinously mismanaged its American policy before the war, or it had disgraced itself by the peace. The " Morning Chronicle," while approving the treaty, declared that the Tories were on this point at odds with their own leaders : [1] " Their attachment to the ministers, though strong, cannot reconcile them to this one step, though surely if they would look back with an impartial eye

[1] The Morning Chronicle, Dec. 30, 1814.

on the imbecility and error with which their idols
conducted the war, they must acknowledge their pru-
dence in putting an end to it. One of them very
honestly said, two days ago, that if they had not put
an end to the war, the war would have put an end to
their Ministry." Whatever doubts existed about the
temper of England before that time, no one doubted
after the peace of Ghent that war with the United
States was an unpopular measure with the British
people.

Nevertheless the "Times" and the Tories continued their complaints until March 9, when two simultaneous pieces of news silenced criticism of the
American treaty. The severe defeat at New Orleans
became known at the moment when Napoleon, having
quitted Elba, began his triumphal return to Paris.
These news, coming in the midst of Corn Riots, silenced further discussion of American relations, and
left ministers free to redeem at Waterloo the failures
they had experienced in America.

In the United States news of peace was slow to
arrive. The British sloop-of-war "Favorite" bore
the despatches, and was still at sea when the month
of February began. The commissioners from Massachusetts and Connecticut, bearing the demands of
the Hartford Convention, started for Washington.
Every one was intent on the situation of New Orleans,
where a disaster was feared. Congress seemed to
have abandoned the attempt to provide means of defence, although it began another effort to create a

bank on Dallas's plan. A large number of the most intelligent citizens believed that two announcements would soon be made, — one, that New Orleans was lost; the other, that the negotiation at Ghent had ended in rupture. Under this double shock, the collapse of the national government seemed to its enemies inevitable.

In this moment of suspense, the first news arrived from New Orleans. To the extreme relief of the Government and the Republican majority in Congress, they learned, February 4, that the British invasion was defeated and New Orleans saved. The victory was welcomed by illuminations, votes of thanks, and rejoicings greater than had followed the more important success at Plattsburg, or the more brilliant battles at Niagara; for the success won at New Orleans relieved the Government from a load of anxiety, and postponed a crisis supposed to be immediately at hand. Half the influence of the Hartford Convention was destroyed by it; and the commissioners, who were starting for the capital, had reason to expect a reception less favorable by far than they would have met had the British been announced as masters of Louisiana. Yet the immediate effect of the news was not to lend new vigor to Congress, but rather to increase its inertness, and to encourage its dependence on militia, Treasury notes, and good fortune.

A week afterward, on the afternoon of Saturday, February 11, the British sloop-of-war " Favorite " sailed up New York harbor, and the city quickly heard rumors of peace. At eight o'clock that evening the American special messenger landed, bringing the official documents intrusted to his care ; and when the news could no longer be doubted, the city burst into an uproar of joy. The messenger was slow in reaching Washington, where he arrived only on the evening of Tuesday, February 13, and delivered his despatches to the Secretary of State.

Had the treaty been less satisfactory than it was, the President would have hesitated long before advising its rejection, and the Senate could hardly have gained courage to reject it. In spite of rumors from London and significant speculations on the London Exchange, known in America in the middle of January, no one had seriously counted on a satisfactory peace, as was proved by the steady depression of government credit and of the prices of American staples. The reaction after the arrival of the news was natural, and so violent that few persons stopped to scrutinize the terms. Contrary to Clay's forebodings, the treaty, mere armistice though it seemed to be, was probably the most popular treaty ever negotiated by the United States. The President sent it to the Senate February 15 ; and the next day, without suggestion of amendment, and apparently without a criticism, unless from Federalists, the Senate unanimously confirmed it, thirty-five senators uniting in approval.

Yet the treaty was not what the Government had

expected in declaring the war, or such as it had a
right to demand. The Republicans admitted it in
private, and the Federalists proclaimed it in the
press.   Senator Gore wrote to Governor Strong: [1]
"The treaty must be deemed disgraceful to the Government who made the war and the peace, and will
be so adjudged by all, after the first effusions of joy
at relief have subsided." Opinions differed widely
on the question where the disgrace belonged, —
whether to the Government who made the war, or
to the people who refused to support it ; but no
one pretended that the terms of peace, as far as
they were expressed in the treaty, were so good as
those repeatedly offered by England more than two
years before.   Yet the treaty was universally welcomed, and not a thought of continued war found
expression.

In New England the peace was received with extravagant delight.   While the government messenger
who carried the official news to Washington made no
haste, a special messenger started from New York at
ten o'clock Saturday night, immediately on the landing of the government messenger, and in thirty-two
hours arrived in Boston.   Probably the distance had
rarely been travelled in less time, for the Boston
"Centinel" announced the expense to be two hundred and twenty-five dollars; and such an outlay was
seldom made for rapidity of travel or news.   As the
messenger passed from town to town he announced

---

[1] Gore to Strong, Feb. 18, 1815; Lodge's Cabot, p. 563.

the tidings to the delighted people.[1] Reaching the
" Centinel " office, at Boston, early Monday morning,
he delivered his bulletin, and a few minutes after it
was published all the bells were set ringing; schools
and shops were closed, and a general holiday taken;
flags were hoisted, the British with the American;
the militia paraded, and in the evening the city was
illuminated.   Yet the terms of peace were wholly
unknown, and the people of Massachusetts had
every reason to fear that their interests were sacrificed for the safety of the Union.   Their rejoicing
over the peace was as unreasoning as their hatred
of the war.

Only along the Canadian frontier where the farm-
ers had for three years made large profits by supplying both armies, the peace was received without
rejoicing.[2] South of New York, although less public
delight was expressed, the relief was probably greater
than in New England.   Virginia had suffered most,
and had felt the blockade with peculiar severity.
A few weeks before the treaty was signed, Jefferson
wrote : [3] —

" By the total annihilation in value of the produce
which was to give me sustenance and independence, I
shall be like Tantalus, — up to the shoulders in water,
yet dying with thirst.   We can make indeed enough to
eat, drink, and clothe ourselves, but nothing for our salt,

[1] Goodrich's Recollections, i. 503–505.
[2] Montreal Herald, March 18, 1815; Niles, viii. 132.
[3] Jefferson to W. Short, Nov. 28, 1814; Works, vi. 398.

iron, groceries, and taxes which must be paid in money.
For what can we raise for the market? Wheat? — we
only give it to our horses, as we have been doing ever
since harvest.   Tobacco? — it is not worth the pipe it
is smoked in."

While all Virginia planters were in this situation
February 13, they awoke February 14 to find flour
worth ten dollars a barrel, and groceries fallen fifty
per cent.   They were once more rich beyond their
wants.

So violent and sudden a change in values had never
been known in the United States.   The New York
market saw fortunes disappear and other fortunes
created in the utterance of a single word.   All imported articles dropped to low prices.   Sugar which
sold Saturday at twenty-six dollars a hundred-weight,
sold Monday at twelve dollars and a half.   Tea sank
from two dollars and a quarter to one dollar a pound;
tin fell from eighty to twenty-five dollars a box; cotton fabrics declined about fifty per cent.   On the
other hand flour, cotton, and the other chief staples
of American produce rose in the same proportion.
Nominally flour was worth seven and a half dollars
on Saturday, though no large amounts could have
been sold; on Monday the price was ten dollars,
and all the wheat in the country was soon sold at
that rate.

Owing to the derangement of currency, these prices
expressed no precise specie value.   The effect of the
peace on the currency was for a moment to restore

an apparent equilibrium. In New York the specie
premium of twenty-two per cent was imagined for
a time to have vanished. In truth, United States
six-per-cents rose in New York from seventy-six to
eighty-eight in paper ; Treasury-notes from ninety-
two to ninety-eight. In Philadelphia, on Saturday,
six-per-cents sold at seventy-five ; on Monday, at
ninety-three. The paper depreciation remained about
twenty per cent in New York, about twenty-four per
cent in Philadelphia, and about thirty per cent in
Baltimore. The true value of six-per-cents was about
sixty-eight; of Treasury notes about seventy-eight,
after the announcement of peace.

As rapidly as possible the blockade was raised, and
ships were hurried to sea with the harvests of three
seasons for cargo; but some weeks still passed before
all the operations of war were closed. The news of
peace reached the British squadron below Mobile in
time to prevent further advance on that place ; but
on the ocean a long time elapsed before fighting
wholly ceased.

Some of the worst disasters as well as the greatest triumphs of the war occurred after the treaty of
peace had been signed. The battle of New Orleans
was followed by the loss of Fort Bowyer. At about
the same time a British force occupied Cumberland
Island on the southern edge of the Georgia coast,
and January 13 attacked the fort at the entrance of
the St. Mary's, and having captured it without loss,
ascended the river the next day to the town of

St. Mary's, which they seized, together with its merchandise and valuable ships in the river. Cockburn established his headquarters on Cumberland Island January 22, and threw the whole State of Georgia into agitation, while he waited the arrival of a brigade with which an attack was to be made on Savannah.

The worst disaster of the naval war occurred January 15, when the frigate "President" — one of the three American forty-fours, under Stephen Decatur, the favorite ocean hero of the American service — suffered defeat and capture within fifty miles of Sandy Hook. No naval battle of the war was more disputed in its merits, although its occurrence in the darkest moments of national depression was almost immediately forgotten in the elation of the peace a few days later.

Secretary Jones retired from the Navy Department Dec. 19, 1814, yielding the direction to B. W. Crowninshield of Massachusetts, but leaving a squadron ready for sea at New York under orders for distant service. The "Peacock" and "Hornet," commanded by Warrington and Biddle, were to sail with a storeship on a long cruise in Indian waters, where they were expected to ravage British shipping from the Cape of Good Hope to the China seas. With them Decatur was to go in the "President," and at the beginning of the new year he waited only an opportunity to slip to sea past the blockading squadron. January 14 a strong westerly wind drove the British

fleet out of sight. The " President " set sail, but in
crossing the bar at night grounded, and continued
for an hour or more to strike heavily, until the tide
and strong wind forced her across. Decatur then
ran along the Long Island coast some fifty miles,
when he changed his course to the southeast, hoping
that he had evaded the blockading squadron. This
course was precisely that which Captain Hayes, com-
manding the squadron, expected;[1] and an hour before daylight the four British ships, standing to the
northward and eastward, sighted the " President,"
standing to the southward and eastward, not more
than two miles on the weather-bow of the " Majestic," — the fifty-six-gun razee commanded by Captain
Hayes.

The British ships promptly made chase. Captain
Hayes's squadron, besides the " Majestic," consisted
of the " Endymion," a fifty-gun frigate, with the
" Pomone " and " Tenedos," frigates like the " Guerriere," " Macedonian," and " Java," armed with eigh-
teen-pound guns. Only from the " Endymion " had
Decatur much to fear, for the " Majestic " was slow
and the other ships were weak ; but the " Endymion " was a fast sailer, and especially adapted to
meet the American frigates. The " Endymion," according to British authority, was about one hundred
and fifty-nine feet in length on the lower deck,
and nearly forty-three feet in extreme breadth ; the

[1] Report of Captain Hayes, Jan. 17, 1815; James, Appendix,
p. clxxx; Niles, viii. 175.

"President," on the same authority, was about one hundred and seventy-three feet in length, and forty-four feet in breadth. The "Endymion" carried twenty-six long twenty-four-pounders on the main deck; the "President" carried thirty. The "Endymion" mounted twenty-two thirty-two pound carronades on the spar deck; the "President" mounted twenty. The "Endymion" had also a long brass eighteen-pounder as a bow-chaser; the "President" a long twenty-four-pounder as a bow-chaser, and another as a stern-chaser. The "Endymion" was short-handed after her losses in action with the "Prince de Neufchatel," and carried only three hundred and forty-six men; the "President" carried four hundred and fifty. The "Endymion" was the weaker ship, probably in the proportion of four to five; but for her immediate purpose she possessed a decisive advantage in superior speed, especially in light winds.

At two o'clock in the afternoon, the "Endymion" had gained so much on the "President" as to begin exchanging shots between the stern and bow-chasers.[1] Soon after five o'clock, as the wind fell, the "Endymion" crept up on the "President's" starboard quarter, and "commenced close action."[2] After bearing the enemy's fire for half an hour without reply, Decatur was obliged to alter his course and accept

---

[1] Log of the "Pomone;" Niles, viii. 133. Log of the "Endymion;" James, p. 427.

[2] Report of Captain Hayes; Niles, viii. 175.

battle, or suffer himself to be crippled.[1] The battle lasted two hours and a half, until eight o'clock, when firing ceased; but at half-past nine, according to the " Pomone's " log, the " Endymion " fired two guns, which the " President " returned with one.[2] According to Decatur's account the " Endymion " lay for half an hour under his stern, without firing, while the " President" was trying to escape. In truth the " Endymion " had no need to fire; she was busy bending new sails, while Decatur's ship, according to his official report, was crippled, and in the want of wind could not escape.

In a letter written by Decatur to his wife immediately after the battle, he gave an account of what followed, as he understood it.[3]

" The ' Endymion,' " he began, . . . " was the leading ship of the enemy. She got close under my quarters and was cutting my rigging without my being able to bring a gun to bear upon her. To suffer this was making my capture certain, and that too without injury to the enemy. I therefore bore up for the ' Endymion ' and engaged her for two hours, when we silenced and beat her off. At this time the rest of the ships had got within two miles of us. We made all the sail we could from them, but it was in vain. In three hours the ' Pomone ' and ' Tenedos ' were alongside, and the ' Majestic ' and ' Endymion ' close to us. All that was now left for me to do was to receive the fire of the nearest ship and surrender."

[1] Decatur's Report of Jan. 18, 1815; Niles, viii. 8.
[2] Log of the " Pomone;" Niles, viii. 133.
[3] Niles, vii. 364.

The "Pomone's" account of the surrender completed the story :[1] —

"At eleven, being within gunshot of the 'President' who was still steering to the eastward under a press of sail, with royal, top-gallant, topmast, and lower studding-sails set, finding how much we outsailed her our studding-sails were taken in, and immediately afterward we luffed to port and fired our starboard broadside. The enemy then also luffed to port, bringing his larboard broadside to bear, which was momentarily expected, as a few minutes previous to our closing her she hoisted a light abaft, which in night actions constitutes the ensign. Our second broadside was fired, and the 'President' still luffing up as if intent to lay us on board, we hauled close to port, bracing the yards up, and setting the mainsail; the broadside was again to be fired into his bows, raking, when she hauled down the light, and we hailed demanding if she had surrendered. The reply was in the affirmative, and the firing immediately ceased. The 'Tenedos,' who was not more than three miles off, soon afterward came up, and assisted the 'Pomone' in securing the prize and removing the prisoners. At three quarters past twelve the 'Endymion' came up, and the 'Majestic' at three in the morning."

Between the account given by Decatur and that of the "Pomone's".log were some discrepancies. In the darkness many mistakes were inevitable; but if each party were taken as the best authority on its own side, the connected story seemed to show that Decatur, after beating off the "Endymion," made

[1] Niles, viii. 133.

every effort to escape, but was impressed by the conviction that if overtaken by the squadron, nothing
was left but to receive the fire of the nearest ship,
and surrender. The night was calm, and the " President " made little headway. At eleven o'clock one
of the pursuing squadron came up, and fired two
broadsides. "Thus situated," reported Decatur, "with
about one fifth of my crew killed and wounded, my
ship crippled, and a more than fourfold force opposed
to me, without a chance of escape left, I deemed it
my duty to surrender."

The official Court of Inquiry on the loss of the
" President " reported, a few months afterward, a
warm approval of Decatur's conduct : [1] —

" We fear that we cannot express in a manner that
will do justice to our feelings our admiration of the
conduct of Commodore Decatur and his officers and
crew. . . . As well during the chase as through his contest with the enemy [he] evinced great judgment and
skill, perfect coolness, the most determined resolution,
and heroic courage."

The high praise thus bestowed was doubtless deserved, since the Court of Inquiry was composed of
persons well qualified to judge ; but Decatur's battle with the " Endymion " was far from repeating
the success of his triumph over the " Macedonian."
Anxious to escape rather than to fight, Decatur in
consequence failed either to escape or resist with effect. The action with the " Endymion " lasted three

hours from the time when the British frigate gained the "President's" quarter. For the first half hour the "President" received the "Endymion's" broadsides without reply. During the last half hour the firing slackened and became intermittent. Yet for two hours the ships were engaged at close range, a part of the time within half musket-shot, in a calm sea, and in a parallel line of sailing.[1] At all times of the battle, the ships were well within point-blank range,[2] which for long twenty-four-pounders and thirty-two-pound carronades was about two hundred and fifty yards.[3] Decatur had needed but an hour and a half to disable and capture the "Macedonian," although a heavy swell disturbed his fire, and at no time were the ships within easy range for grape, which was about one hundred and fifty yards. The "Endymion" was a larger and better ship than the "Macedonian," but the "President" was decidedly less efficient than the "United States."

According to Captain Hope's report, the "Endymion" lost eleven men killed and fourteen wounded. The "President" reported twenty-five killed and sixty wounded. Of the two ships the "President" was probably the most severely injured.[4] The masts of both were damaged, and two days afterward both

[1] Log of the "Endymion;" James, p. 428.

[2] Cooper's Naval History, ii. 466.

[3] Adye's Bombardier, p. 197.   Douglas's Naval Gunnery (Fourth edition), p. 103.

[4] Report of Injuries received by the "President;" James, Appendix, p. cxciv, no. 107.

were dismasted in a gale; but while the " President "
lost all her masts by the board, the " Endymion " lost
only her fore and main masts considerably above deck.
On the whole, the injury inflicted by the " President "
on the " Endymion " was less than in proportion to
her relative strength, or to the length of time occupied in the action.   Even on the supposition that the
" President's " fire was directed chiefly against the
" Endymion's " rigging, the injury done was not pro-
portional to the time occupied in doing it.   According to the " Pomone's " log, the " Endymion " **was**
able to rejoin the squadron at quarter before one
o'clock in the night.   According to the " Endymion's " log, she repaired damages in an hour, and
resumed the chase at nine o'clock.[1]

The British ships were surprised that Decatur
should have surrendered to the " Pomone " without
firing a shot.   Apparently the " Pomone's " broadside did little injury, and the " Tenedos " was not
yet in range when the " Pomone " opened fire.   The
question of the proper time to surrender was to be
judged by professional rules; and if resistance was
hopeless, Decatur was doubtless justified in striking when he did; but his apparent readiness to do
so hardly accorded with the popular conception of
his character.

As usual the sloops were more fortunate than
the frigate, and got to sea successfully, January 22,
in a gale of wind which enabled them to run the

[1] James's Naval Occurrences, p. 129.

blockade. Their appointed rendezvous was Tristan
d'Acunha. There the "Hornet" arrived on the morning of March 23, and before she had time to an-
chor sighted the British sloop-of-war "Penguin," —
a new brig then cruising in search of the American
privateer "Young Wasp."

Captain Biddle of the "Hornet" instantly made
chase, and Captain Dickinson of the "Penguin" bore
up and stood for the enemy. According to British
authority the vessels differed only by a "trifling dis-
parity of force."[1] In truth the American was somewhat superior in size, metal, and crew, although not
so decisively as in most of the sloop battles. The
"Hornet" carried eighteen thirty-two-pound carronades and two long twelve-pounders ; the "Penguin"
carried sixteen thirty-two-pound carronades, two long
guns differently reported as twelve-pounders and six-
pounders, and a twelve-pound carronade. The crews
were apparently the same in number, — about one
hundred and thirty-two men. Captain Dickinson had
equipped his vessel especially for the purpose of cap-
turing heavy privateers, and was then looking for
the "Young Wasp," — a vessel decidedly superior to
the "Hornet."[2] Although he had reason to doubt
his ability to capture the "Young Wasp," he did
not fear a combat with the "Hornet," and showed
his confidence by brushing up close alongside and

[1] James, p. 498.

[2] Admiral Tyler to Captain Dickinson, Jan. 31, 1815; Niles,
viii. 345.

firing a gun, while the " Hornet," all aback, waited
for him.

The result was very different from that of Decatur's two-hour battle with the " Endymion." In little
more than twenty minutes of close action the " Penguin's " foremast and bowsprit were gone, her captain killed, and thirty-eight men killed or wounded,
or more than one fourth the crew. The brig was
" a perfect wreck," according to the British official
report, when the senior surviving officer hailed and
surrendered.[1] The " Hornet " was not struck in
the hull, but was very much cut up in rigging and
spars. She had two killed, and nine wounded. " It
was evident," said Captain Biddle's report, " that
our fire was greatly superior both in quickness and
effect."

The " Penguin " was destroyed, and the " Hornet "
and " Peacock " continued their cruise until April
27, when they chased for twenty-four hours a strange
sail, which proved to be the British seventy-four
" Cornwallis." On discovering the character of the
chase Biddle made off to windward, but found that
the enemy " sailed remarkably fast and was very
weatherly." At daylight of the 29th, the " Cornwallis " was within gunshot on the " Hornet's " lee-
quarter. Her shot did not take effect, and Biddle,
by lightening his ship, drew out of fire; but a
few hours later the enemy again came up within

[1] Report of Lieutenant McDonald, April 6, 1815 ; James,
Appendix, p. cc, no. 111.

three quarters of a mile, in a calm sea, and opened once more. Three shot struck the " Hornet," but without crippling her. Biddle threw over everything that could be spared, except one long gun; and a fortunate change of wind enabled him a second time to creep out of fire. He escaped; but the loss of his guns, anchors, cables, and boats obliged him to make for San Salvador, where he heard the news of peace.[1]

Captain Warrington in the " Peacock " continued his cruise to the Indian Ocean, and captured four Indiamen. In the Straits of Sunda, June 30, he encountered a small East India Company's cruiser, whose commander hailed and announced peace. Warrington replied, " directing him at the same time to haul his colors down if it were the case, in token of it, — adding that if he did not, I should fire into him." The brig refused to strike its colors, and Warrington nearly destroyed her by a broadside.[2] For this violence little excuse could be offered, for the " Nautilus " was not half the " Peacock's " strength, and could not have escaped. Warrington, like most officers of the American navy, remembered the " Chesapeake " too well.

The cruise of the " President," " Peacock," and " Hornet " ended in the loss of the " President," the disabling of the " Hornet," and the arrival of the " Peacock " alone at the point intended for their

---

[1] Biddle's Report of June 10, 1815; Niles, viii. 438.
[2] Warrington's Letter of Nov. 11, 1815; Niles, x. 58.

common cruising-ground. No other national vessels were at sea after peace was signed, except the " Constitution," which late in December sailed from Boston under the command of Captain Charles Stewart, — a Philadelphian of Irish descent, not thirty-nine years old, but since 1806 a captain in the United States service.

Cruising between Gibraltar and Madeira, at about one o'clock on the afternoon of February 20 Captain Stewart discovered two sail ahead, which he chased and overtook at six o'clock. Both were ship-rigged sloops-of-war. The larger of the two was the " Cyane." Americans preferred to call her a frigate, but that designation, though vague at best, could hardly be applied to such a vessel. The " Cyane " was a frigate-built sloop-of-war, or corvette, like the " Little Belt," carrying a regular complement of one hundred and eighty-five men. Her length on the lower deck was one hundred and eighteen feet ; her breadth was thirty-two feet. She carried thirty-three guns, all carronades except two long-nines or twelves. Her companion, the " Levant," was also a sloop-of-war of the larger sort, though smaller than the " Cyane." She mounted twenty-one guns, all carronades except two long nine-pounders. Her regular crew was one hundred and thirty-five men and boys.

Either separately or together the British ships were decidedly unequal to the " Constitution," which could, by remaining at long range, sink them both without receiving a shot in return. The " Constitution " carried thirty-two long twenty-four-pounders; while the two sloops could reply to these guns only by four long nine-pounders. The "Constitution" carried four hundred and fifty men; the two sloops at the time of the encounter carried three hundred and thirty-six seamen, marines, and officers.[1] The "Constitution" was built of great strength; the two sloops had only the frames of their class. The utmost that the British captains could hope was that one of the two vessels might escape by the sacrifice of the other.

Instead of escaping, the senior officer, Captain George Douglass of the "Levant," resolved to engage the frigate, "in the hopes, by disabling her, to prevent her intercepting two valuable convoys that sailed from Gibraltar about the same time as the 'Levant' and 'Cyane.'"[2] Captain Douglass knew his relative strength, for he had heard that the American frigate was on his course.[3] Yet he seriously expected to disable her, and made a courageous attempt to do so.

The two ships, close together, tried first for the weather-gauge, but the "Constitution" outsailed them also on that point. They then bore up in hope of delaying the engagement till night, but the "Constitution" overhauled them too rapidly for the success

[1] Statement of the actual force, etc., Stewart's Report; Niles, viii. 219.

[2] James, Naval Occurrences, p. 458.

[3] James, Naval Occurrences, p. 458.

of that plan. They then stood on the starboard tack, the " Cyane " astern, the " Levant " a half-cable length ahead, while the " Constitution " came up to windward and opened fire. Commodore Stewart's report described the result:[1] —

" At five minutes past six ranged up on the starboard side of the sternmost ship [the ' Cyane '], about three hundred yards distant, and commenced the action by broadsides, — both ships returning our fire with great spirit for about fifteen minutes. Then the fire of the enemy beginning to slacken, and the great column of smoke collected under our lee, induced us to cease our fire to ascertain their positions and conditions. In about three minutes the smoke clearing away, we found ourselves abreast of the headmost ship [the ' Levant '], the sternmost ship luffing up for our larboard quarter."

Three hundred yards was a long range for carronades, especially in British sloops whose marksmanship was indifferent at best. According to the British court-martial on the officers of the " Cyane " and " Levant," their carronades had little effect.[2] If Stewart managed his ship as his duty required, the two sloops until that moment should have been allowed to make little effective return of the " Constitution's " broadside of sixteen twenty-four-pounders except by two nine-pounders. They were in the position of the " Essex " at Valparaiso. The " Cyane " naturally luffed up, in order to bring her carronades

[1] Minutes of the Action; Niles, viii. 219.

[2] Niles, viii. 363. Cf. Letter of Lieutenant Shubrick; Niles, viii. 383.

to bear, but she was already cut to pieces, and made the matter worse by closing.

" We poured a broadside into the headmost ship," continued the American account, " and then braced aback our main and mizzen topsails and backed astern under cover of the smoke abreast the sternmost ship, when the action was continued with spirit and considerable effect until thirty-five minutes past six, when the enemy's fire again slackened."

The " Levant," after receiving two stern-raking fires, bore up at forty minutes past six and began to repair damages two miles to leeward. The " Cyane," having become unmanageable, struck at ten minutes before seven. The most remarkable incident of the battle occurred after the " Cyane " struck, when the " Constitution " went after the " Levant " which was in sight to leeward. The little " Levant," instead of running away, stood directly for the huge American frigate, more than three times her size, and ranging close alongside fired a broadside into her as the two ships passed on opposite tacks. Although the sloop received the " Constitution's " broadside in return, she was only captured at last after an hour's chase, at ten o'clock, much cut up in spars and rigging, but still sea-worthy, and with seven men killed and sixteen wounded, or only one casualty to six of her crew.

In truth, the injury inflicted by the " Constitution's " fire was not so great as might have been expected. The " Cyane " lost twelve killed and

twenty-six wounded, if the American report was
correct. Neither ship was dismasted or in a sink-
ing condition. Both arrived safely, March 10, at
Porto Praya. On the other hand, the "Constitution" was struck eleven times in the hull, and lost
three men killed and twelve wounded, three of the
latter mortally. She suffered more than in her battle with the "Guerriere," — a result creditable to
the British ships, considering that in each case the
"Constitution" could choose her own range.

Stewart took his prizes to the Cape de Verde
Islands. At noon, March 11, while lying in port at
Porto Praya, three British frigates appeared off the
harbor, and Stewart instantly stood to sea, passing
the enemy's squadron to windward within gunshot.
The three frigates made chase, and at one o'clock,
as the "Cyane" was dropping astern, Stewart signalled to her to tack ship, and either escape, if not
pursued, or return to Porto Praya. The squadron
paid no attention to the "Cyane," but followed the
"Constitution" and "Levant." At three o'clock,
the "Levant" falling behind, Stewart signalled her
also to tack. Immediately the whole British squadron abandoned pursuit of the "Constitution" and
followed the "Levant" to Porto Praya, where they
seized her under the guns of the Portuguese batteries.
Meanwhile the "Constitution" and "Cyane" escaped,
and reached the United States without further accident. The extraordinary blunders of the British
squadron were never satisfactorily explained.

These combats and cruises, with the last ravages of the privateers, closed the war on the ocean as it had long ceased on land; and meanwhile the people of the United States had turned their energies to undertakings of a wholly different character.

CHAPTER IV.

THE long, exciting, and splendid panorama of revolution and war, which for twenty-five years absorbed the world's attention and dwarfed all other interests, vanished more quickly in America than in Europe, and left fewer elements of disturbance. The transformation scene of a pantomime was hardly more sudden or complete than the change that came over the United States at the announcement of peace. In a single day, almost in a single instant, the public turned from interests and passions that had supplied its thought for a generation, and took up a class of ideas that had been unknown or but vaguely defined before.

At Washington the effect of the news was so extraordinary as to shake faith in the seriousness of party politics. Although the peace affected in no way party doctrine or social distinctions, a new epoch for the Union began from the evening of February 13, when the messenger from Ghent arrived with the treaty. No one stopped to ask why a government, which was discredited and falling to pieces at one moment, should appear as a successful and even a glorious national representative a moment afterward.

Politicians dismissed the war from their thoughts, as they dismissed the treaty, with the single phrase : "Not an inch ceded or lost!"[1] The commissioners from Massachusetts and Connecticut who appeared at Washington with the recommendations of the Hartford Convention, returned home as quietly as possible, pursued by the gibes of the press. The war was no more popular then than it had been before, as the subsequent elections proved; but the danger was passed, and passion instantly subsided.

Only by slow degrees the country learned to appreciate the extraordinary feat which had been performed, not so much by the people as by a relatively small number of individuals. Had a village rustic, with one hand tied behind his back, challenged the champion of the prize-ring, and in three or four rounds obliged him to draw the stakes, the result would have been little more surprising than the result of the American campaign of 1814. The most intelligent and best educated part of society both in the United States and in Great Britain could not believe it, and the true causes of British defeat remained a subject of conjecture and angry dispute. The enemies of the war admitted only that peace had saved Madison ; but this single concession, which included many far-reaching consequences, was granted instantly, and from that moment the national government triumphed over all its immediate dangers.

[1] Ingersoll, ii. 311.

While the Senate unanimously ratified the treaty February 16, the House set to work with much more alacrity than was its habit to dispose of the business before it. Haste was necessary. Barely fourteen days remained before the Thirteenth Congress should expire, and in that interval some system of peace legislation must be adopted. The struggle over the proposed Bank charter was still raging, for the Senate had passed another bill of incorporation February 11, over which the House was occupied the whole day of February 13 in a sharp and close contest. The first effect of the peace was to stop this struggle. By a majority of one vote, seventy-four to seventy-three, February 17, the House laid the subject aside.

Three days afterward, February 20, the President sent to Congress a Message transmitting the treaty with its ratifications, and congratulating the country on the close of a war " waged with the success which is the natural result of the wisdom of the legislative councils, of the patriotism of the people, of the public spirit of the militia, and of the valor of the military and naval forces of the country." After recommending to Congress the interests of the soldiers and sailors, the Message passed to the reduction of expenditures, which required immediate attention :

" There are, however," continued Madison, " important considerations which forbid a sudden and general revocation of the measures that have been produced by the war. Experience has taught us that neither the pacific dispositions of the American people, nor the pa-

cific character of their political institutions, can altogether
exempt them from that strife which appears, beyond the
ordinary lot of nations, to be incident to the actual period
of the world ; and the same faithful monitor demon-
strates that a certain degree of preparation for war is
not only indispensable to avert disasters in the onset,
but affords also the best security for the continuance
of peace."

The avowal that experience had shown the error of
the principle adopted by the nation in 1801 was not
confined to President Madison. Monroe spoke even
more plainly. In a letter to the military committee,
February 24, Monroe urged that an army of twenty
thousand men should be retained on the peace establishment. Each soldier of the rank-and-file was supposed to cost in peace about two hundred dollars a
year, and Monroe's proposal involved an annual
expense of more than five million dollars.

As far as concerned Madison and Monroe the repu-
diation of old Republican principles seemed complete ;
but the people had moved less rapidly than their leaders. Had Congress, while debating the subject February 25, known that Napoleon was then quitting
Elba to seize once more the control of France, and
to rouse another European convulsion with all its possible perils to neutrals, the President's views might
have been adopted without serious dispute ; but in
the absence of evident danger, an army of twenty
thousand men seemed unnecessary. The finances
warranted no such extravagance. Dallas wrote to

Eppes, the chairman of the Ways and Means Committee, a letter [1] dated February 20, sketching a temporary financial scheme for the coming year. He proposed to fund at seven per cent the outstanding Treasury notes, amounting to $18,637,000 ; and even after thus sweeping the field clear of pressing claims, he still required the extravagant war-taxes in order to meet expenses, and depended on a further issue of Treasury notes, or a loan, to support the peace establishments of the army and navy. The state of the currency was desperate, and the revenue for the year 1815 was estimated at $18,200,000 in the notes of State banks, — a sum little in excess of the estimated civil necessities.

The military committee of the House showed no sympathy with the new principles urged upon Congress by the Executive. Troup of Georgia reported a bill, February 22, fixing the peace establishment at ten thousand men, with two major-generals and four brigadiers. In submitting this proposal, Troup urged the House, February 25, to accept the reduction to ten thousand as the lowest possible standard, requiring only the expense of two and a half millions ; but no sooner did he take his seat than Desha of Kentucky moved to substitute " six " for " ten," and a vigorous debate followed, ending in the adoption of Desha's amendment in committee by a majority of nineteen votes. The war leaders were greatly annoyed by this new triumph of the peace party. As a

[1] Annals of Congress, 1814–1815 ; iii. 1178.

matter of principle, the vote on Desha's amendment affirmed Jefferson's pacific system and condemned the Federalist heresies of Madison and Monroe. The war leaders could not acquiesce in such a decision, and rallying for another effort, February 27, they remonstrated hotly. Forsyth of Georgia was particularly emphatic in defining the issue: [1] —

"He had hoped that the spirit of calculation falsely styled economy, whose contracted view was fixed upon present expense, and was incapable of enlarging it to permanent and eventual advantage, had been laid forever by the powerful exorcisms of reason and experience. It would seem however that it had been only lulled by the presence of a more powerful demon. Since the potent spell of necessity had been broken, the troubled spirit of petty calculation was again awakened to vex the counsels and destroy the best hopes of the country."

For three years the friends of strong government, under the pressure of war, had been able to drive Congress more or less in their own direction; but at the announcement of peace their power was greatly lessened, and their unwilling associates were no longer disposed to follow their lead or to tolerate their assumptions of superiority. Desha retaliated in the tone of 1798: —

"Do they suppose that the House do not understand the subject; or do they suppose that by this great flow of eloquence they can make the substantial part of the House change their opinions in so short a time? When I speak of the substantial part of the House, I mean

[1] Annals of Congress, 1814–1815, pp. 1213, 1250.

those who think much and speak but little; who make
common-sense their guide, and not theoretical or visionary projects. . . . Some gentlemen advocate ten thousand and others twenty thousand of a standing army.
The policy is easy to be seen through. The advocates
of a perpetual system of taxation discover that if they
cannot retain a considerable standing army, they will
have no good plea for riveting the present taxes on
the people."

In the process of national growth, public opinion
had advanced since 1801 several stages in its development; but the speeches of Forsyth, Calhoun, and
Lowndes on one side, like that of Desha on the other,
left still in doubt the amount of change. While
Forsyth admitted that he had under-estimated the
strength of the economical spirit, Desha certainly
over-estimated the force of the men "who think
much and speak but little." With Federalist assistance, Desha's friends passed the bill for an army
of six thousand men by a vote of seventy-five to
sixty-five; but the Senate, by a more decided vote
of eighteen to ten, substituted "fifteen" for "six."
With this amendment the bill was returned to the
House March 2, which by an almost unanimous vote
refused to concur. The bill was sent to a conference
committee, which reported the original plan of ten
thousand men; and in the last hours of the session,
March 3, the House yielded. By a vote of seventy
to thirty-eight the peace establishment was fixed at
ten thousand men.

The movement of public opinion was more evident in regard to the navy. Instead of repeating the experiments of 1801, Congress maintained the whole war establishment, and appropriated four million dollars chiefly for the support of frigates and ships-of-the-line. The vessels on the Lakes were dismantled and laid up; the gunboats, by an Act approved February 27, were ordered to be sold; but the sum of two hundred thousand dollars was appropriated for the annual purchase of ship-timber during the next three years, and the whole navy thenceforward consisted of cruisers, which were to be kept as far as possible in active service. As the first task of the new ships, an Act, approved March 3, authorized hostilities against the Dey of Algiers, who had indulged in the plunder of American commerce.

These hasty arrangements for the two services, coupled with an equally hasty financial makeshift, completed the career of the Thirteenth Congress, which expired March 4, as little admired or regretted as the least popular of its predecessors. Not upon Congress but upon the Executive Departments fell the burden of peace as of war, and on the Executive the new situation brought many embarrassments.

The first and most delicate task of the Government was the reduction of the army. No one could greatly blame Monroe for shrinking from the invidious duty of dismissing two thirds of the small force which had sustained so well and with so little support the character of the country; but the haste which he showed in leaving the War Department suggested also how keenly he must have suffered under its burdens. His name was sent to the Senate, February 27, as Secretary of State; no Secretary of War was nominated, but Dallas, with the courage that marked his character, undertook to manage the War Department as well as the Treasury until the necessary arrangements for the new army should be made.

April 8 Dallas wrote to six generals, — Brown, Jackson, Scott, Gaines, Macomb, and Ripley, — requesting their attendance at Washington to report a plan for the new army. Jackson and Gaines were unable to attend. The rest of the board reported a scheme dividing the country into two military districts, north and south; and into nine departments, five in the northern, four in the southern division, — allotting to each the troops needed for its service. May 17 the new arrangements were announced. Brown was ordered to command the northern district, with Ripley and Macomb as brigadiers. Jackson took the southern district, with Scott and Gaines as brigadiers. Eight regiments of infantry, one of riflemen, and one of light artillery were retained, together with the corps of artillery and engineers. As far as possible, all the officers whose names became famous for a generation received rank and reward.

No such operation was necessary for the navy, where no reduction was required. In the civil service, Madison enjoyed the satisfaction of rewarding the friends who had stood by him in his trials. Feb-

ruary 27 he sent to the Senate, with the nomination
of Monroe as Secretary of State, the name of J. Q.
Adams as Minister to England. At the same time
Bayard was appointed to St. Petersburg, and Gallatin
to Paris. The nomination of Bayard proved to be an
empty compliment, for he arrived, August 1, in the
Delaware River, in the last stages of illness, and was
carried ashore the next day only to die.

These appointments were well received and readily
confirmed by the Senate; but Madison carried favorit-
ism too far for the Senate's approval when, March 1,
he nominated Major-General Dearborn to be Secretary of War. Dearborn had few or no enemies, but
the distinction thus shown him roused such strong
remonstrance that Madison hastened to recall the
nomination, and substituted Crawford in Dearborn's
place. The Senate had already rejected Dearborn,
but consented to erase the record from their journal,[1]
and Crawford became Secretary of War.

Thus the government in all its branches glided into
the new conditions, hampered only by the confusion
of the currency, which could not be overcome. The
people were even more quick than the government
to adapt themselves to peace. In New Orleans alone
a few weeks of alarm were caused by extraordinary
acts of arbitrary power on the part of General Jackson during the interval before the peace became officially known; but public order was not seriously dis-

[1] Madison to Dearborn, March 4, 1815; Madison's Works,
ii. 598.

turbed, and the civil authority was restored March 13.
Elsewhere the country scarcely stopped to notice the
cost or the consequences of the war.

In truth the cost was moderate. Measured by loss
of life in battle, it was less than that reported in
many single battles fought by Napoleon. An army
which never exceeded thirty thousand effectives, or
placed more than four thousand regular rank-and-file
in a single action, could not sacrifice many lives. According to the received estimates the number of men
killed in battle on land did not much exceed fifteen
hundred, including militia, while the total of killed
and wounded little exceeded five thousand.[1] Sick-
ness was more fatal than wounds, but a population of
eight millions felt camp-diseases hardly more than its
periodical malarial fevers.

The precise financial cost of the war, measured only
by increase of debt, was equally moderate. During
three years, — from February, 1812, until February,
1815, — the government sold six per cent bonds at
various rates of discount, to the amount of fifty
million dollars, and this sum was the limit of its
loans, except for a few bank discounts of Treasury
notes not exceeding a million in all. By forcing
Treasury notes on its creditors the Treasury obtained
the use of twenty millions more. After the peace it
issued bonds and new Treasury notes, which raised
the aggregate amount of war debt, as far as could
be ascertained, to about eighty million five hundred

[1] Niles, x. 154.

thousand dollars, which was the war-addition to the old nominal capital of debt, and increased the total indebtedness to one hundred and twenty-seven millions at the close of the year 1815.[1]

The debt had exceeded eighty millions twenty years before, and in the interval the country had greatly increased its resources. The war debt was a trifling load, and would not have been felt except for the confusion of the currency and the unnecessary taxation imposed at the last moments of the war. That the currency and the war taxes were severe trials was not to be denied, but of other trials the people had little to complain.

Considering the dangers to which the United States were exposed, they escaped with surprising impunity. The shores of Chesapeake Bay and of Georgia were plundered; but the British government paid for the slaves carried away, and no town of importance except Washington was occupied by an enemy. Contrary to the usual experience of war, the richest parts of the country suffered least. Only the Niagara frontier was systematically ravaged. When the blockade of the coast was raised, every seaboard city was able instantly to resume its commercial habits without having greatly suffered from the interruption. The harvests of two seasons were ready for immediate export, and the markets of Europe were waiting to receive them. Every man found occupation, and capital instantly returned to its old channels. From the

[1] Dallas's Report of Dec. 6, 1815; State Papers, Finance, iii. 8.

moment of peace the exports of domestic produce
began to exceed five million dollars a month, while
four millions was the highest average for any previous twelvemonth, and the average for the seven
years of embargo and blockade since 1807 fell much
short of two and a half millions. The returns of
commerce and navigation showed that during the
seven months from March 1 to October 1, 1815,
domestic produce valued at forty-six million dollars
was exported, and American shipping to the amount
of eight hundred and fifty-four thousand tons was
employed in the business of export.[1]

The ease and rapidity of this revolution not only
caused the war to be quickly forgotten, but also
silenced political passions.   For the first time in
their history as a nation, the people of the United
States ceased to disturb themselves about politics or
patronage.   Every political principle was still open
to dispute, and was disputed; but prosperity put an
end to faction.   No evidence could be given to prove
that the number or weight of persons who held the
opinions commonly known as Federalist, diminished
either then or afterward.   Massachusetts showed no
regret for the attitude she had taken.   At the April
election, six weeks after the proclamation of peace,
although Samuel Dexter was the Republican candidate, the State still gave to Governor Strong a
majority of about seven thousand in a total vote of
ninety-five thousand.   The Federalists reasonably

[1] State Papers, Commerce and Navigation, ii. 647.

regarded this vote as an express approval of the
Hartford Convention and its proposed measures, and
asked what would have been their majority had
peace not intervened to save the Government from
odium.   They believed not only that their popular
support would have been greater, but that it would
also have shown a temper beyond control; yet the
Federalist majority in April was no longer hostile to
the Government.

The other elections bore the same general character.   Even .in New York the popular reaction seemed
rather against the war than in its favor.   New York
city in April returned Federalist members to the
State legislature, causing a tie in the Assembly, each
party controlling sixty-three votes.[1]   In Virginia the
peace produced no change so decided as to warrant
a belief that the war had become popular.   In April
John Randolph defeated Eppes and recovered control
of his district.   The State which had chosen sixteen Republicans and seven opposition congressmen
in 1813, elected in 1815 seventeen Republicans and
six opposition members.   The stability of parties was
the more remarkable in New York and Virginia, because those States were first to feel the effects of
renewed prosperity.

After the excitement of peace was past, as the
summer drew toward a close, economical interests
dwarfed the old political distinctions and gave a new
character to parties.   A flood of wealth poured into

[1] Hammond, i. 401.

the Union at a steady rate of six or seven million
dollars a month, and the distribution of so large a
sum could not fail to show interesting results.   The
returns soon proved that the larger portion belonged
to the Southern States.   Cotton, at a valuation of
twenty cents a pound, brought seventeen and a half
millions to the planters; tobacco brought eight and
a quarter millions; rice produced nearly two million
eight hundred thousand dollars.   Of fifty millions received from abroad in payment for domestic produce
within seven or eight months after the peace, the
slave States probably took nearly two thirds, though
the white population of the States south of the Potomac was less than half the white population of the
Union.   The stimulus thus given to the slave system
was violent, and was most plainly shown in the cotton States, where at least twenty million dollars were
distributed in the year 1815 among a white population hardly exceeding half a million in all, while
the larger portion fell to the share of a few slave-
owners.[1]

Had the Northern States shared equally in the
effects of this stimulus, the situation would have
remained relatively as before; but the prosperity of
the North was only moderate.   The chief export
of the Northern States was wheat and Indian corn.
Even of these staples, Maryland and Virginia furnished a share; yet the total value of the wheat and
corn exported from the Union was but eight million

[1] State Papers, Commerce and Navigation, ii. 23.

three hundred and fifty thousand dollars, while that
of tobacco alone was eight and a quarter millions.
While flour sold at nine or ten dollars a barrel,
and Napoleon's armies were vying with the Russians
and Austrians in creating an artificial demand, the
Middle States made a fair profit from their crops,
although much less than was made by the tobacco and cotton planters ; but New England produced little for export, and there the peace brought
only ruin.

Ordinarily shipping was the source of New England's profits. For twenty-five years the wars in
Europe had given to New England shipping advantages which ceased with the return of peace. At
first the change of condition was not felt, for every
ship was promptly employed ; but the reappearance
of foreign vessels in American harbors showed that
competition must soon begin, and that the old rates
of profit were at an end.

Had this been all, Massachusetts could have borne
it ; but the shipping on the whole suffered least among
New England interests. The new manufactures, in
which large amounts of capital had been invested,
were ruined by the peace. If the United States
poured domestic produce valued at fifty million dollars into the markets of Great Britain, Great Britain
and her dependencies poured in return not less than
forty million dollars' worth of imports into the United
States, and inundated the Union with manufactured
goods which were sold at any sacrifice to relieve the

British markets. Although the imported manufactures paid duties of twenty-five per cent or more, they were sold at rates that made American competition impossible.

The cotton manufacturers of Rhode Island, in a memorial to Congress, dated October 20, 1815, declared that their one hundred and forty manufactories, operating one hundred and thirty thousand spindles, could no longer be worked with profit, and were threatened with speedy destruction.[1] New England could foresee with some degree of certainty the ultimate loss of the great amount of capital invested in these undertakings; but whether such fears for the future were just or not, the loss of present profits was not a matter of speculation, but of instant and evident notoriety. Before the close of the year 1815 little profit was left to the new industries. The cotton manufacture, chiefly a New England interest, was supposed to employ a capital of forty million dollars, and to expend about fifteen millions a year in wages.[2] The woollen manufacture, largely in Connecticut, was believed to employ a capital of twelve million dollars.[3] Most of the large factories for these staples were altogether stopped.

From every quarter the peace brought distress upon New England. During the war most of the

---

[1] Annals of Congress, 1815–1816, p. 1651.

[2] Report on Manufactures, Feb. 13, 1816; Niles ix. 447.

[3] Report on Woollen Manufactures, March 6, 1816; Niles, x. 82.

richer prizes had been sent to New England ports, and the sale of their cargoes brought money and buyers into the country ; but this monopoly ceased at the same moment with the monopoly of manufactures. The lumber trade was almost the last surviving interest of considerable value, but in November Parliament imposed duties on American lumber which nearly destroyed the New England trade. The fisheries alone seemed to remain as a permanent resource.

The effect of these changes from prosperity to adversity was shown in the usual forms. Emigration became active. Thousands of native New Englanders transferred themselves to the valley of the Mohawk and Western New York. All the cities of the coast had suffered a check from the war ; but while New York and Philadelphia began to recover their lost ground, Boston was slow to feel the impulse. The financial reason could be partly seen in the bank returns of Massachusetts. In January, 1814, the Massachusetts banks held about $7,300,000 in specie.[1] In January and February, 1815, when peace was declared, the same banks probably held still more specie, as the causes which led to the influx were not removed. In June, about three months later, they held only $3,464,000 in specie, and the drain steadily continued, until in June, 1816, the specie in their vaults was reduced to $1,260,000, while their

[1] Niles's Articles on the New England Convention, Dec. 8, 1814; Niles, vii. 196.

discounts were not increased and their circulation was diminished.[1]

The state of the currency and the policy pursued by the Treasury added to the burden carried by New England. There alone the banks maintained specie payments. In the autumn of 1815, while the notes of the Boston banks were equivalent to gold, Treasury notes were at eleven per cent discount in Boston; New York bank-notes were at eleven and a half per cent discount; Philadelphia at sixteen; Baltimore at seventeen and eighteen; and United States six-per-cent bonds sold at eighty-six. In New England the Government exacted payments either in Treasury notes or in the notes of local banks equivalent to specie. Elsewhere it accepted the notes of local banks at a rate of depreciation much greater than that of Treasury notes. This injustice in exacting taxes was doubled by an equivalent injustice in paying debts. In New England the Treasury compelled creditors to take payment in whatever medium it had at hand, or to go unpaid. Elsewhere the Treasury paid its debts in the currency it received for its taxes.

Dallas admitted the wrong, but made no serious attempt to correct it. So complicated was the currency that the Treasury was obliged to keep four accounts with each of its ninety-four banks of deposit, — (1) in the currency of the bank itself; (2) in

[1] Schedule etc.; Massachusetts Senate Document, No. 38, Jan. 17, 1838.

special deposits of other bank currency; (3) in special deposits of Treasury notes bearing interest; (4) in small Treasury notes not bearing interest. In New England, and also in the cities of New York and Philadelphia, for some months after the peace the taxes were paid in Treasury notes. So little local currency was collected at these chief centres of business that the Treasury did not attempt to discharge its warrants there in currency. As the Treasury notes gradually appreciated in value above the local bank-notes of the Middle States, tax-payers ceased to make payments in them, and paid in their local bank-notes. Little by little the accumulation of local currency in the Treasury deposits at Philadelphia and New York increased, until the Treasury was able to draw on them in payment of its warrants; but even at those points this degree of credit was not attained in 1815, and in New England the Treasury still made no payments except in Treasury notes, or the notes of distant banks at a discount still greater than that of Treasury notes. This exceptional severity toward New England was admitted by Dallas, and excused only for the reason that if he were just to New England he must be severe to the rest of the country. Every holder of a Treasury warrant would have demanded payment at the place where the local medium was of the highest value, which was Boston; and as the Treasury could not pay specie at Boston without exacting specie elsewhere, Dallas paid no attention to Constitutional scruples or legal objections, but arbitrarily excluded Boston from the number of points where warrants were paid in local currency.[1]

The people of Boston criticised, with much severity and with apparent justice, Dallas's management of the finances, which seemed to require some explanation not furnished in his reports. By an Act approved March 3, Congress authorized a loan of $18,452,800 to absorb the outstanding Treasury notes. At that time, under the momentary reaction of peace excitement, Treasury notes were supposed to be worth about ninety-four cents in the dollar, and Dallas expected to convert them nearly dollar for dollar into six-per-cent bonds. His proposals were issued March 10, inviting bids for twelve millions, and requiring only " that the terms of the proposals should bear some relation to the actual fair price of stock in the market of Philadelphia or New York." When the bids were received, Dallas rejected them all, because in his opinion they were below the market rates. " In point of fact," he afterward said, " no direct offer was made to subscribe at a higher rate than eighty-nine per cent, while some of the offers were made at a rate even lower than seventy-five per cent." Although the old six-per-cents were then selling at eighty-nine, eighty-eight, and eighty-seven in Boston and New York, Dallas held that " the real condition of the public credit " required him to insist upon ninety-five as the value of the new stock.

[1] Dallas's Report of Dec. 3, 1816; State Papers, Finance, iii. 130.

After failing to obtain ninety-five or even ninety as the price of his bonds, Dallas resorted to expedients best described in his own words. As he could not fund the Treasury notes at the rate he wished, he abandoned the attempt, and used the loan only to supply the local wants of the Treasury : —

"The objects of the loan being to absorb a portion of the Treasury-note debt, and to acquire a sufficiency of local currency for local purposes, the price of the stock at the Treasury was of course independent of the daily up-and-down prices of the various stock markets in the Union, and could only be affected by the progress toward the attainment of those objects. Thus while the wants of the Treasury were insufficiently supplied, offers to subscribe were freely accepted, and the parties were sometimes authorized and invited to increase the amount of their offers ; but where the local funds had so accumulated as to approach the probable amount of the local demands, the price of the stock was raised at the Treasury, and when the accumulation was deemed adequate to the whole amount of the local demands the loan was closed." [1]

Governments which insisted upon borrowing at rates higher than the money market allowed, could do so only by helping to debase the currency. Dallas's course offered encouragement to the suspended banks alone. The schedule of his loans proved that he paid a premium to insolvency. Of all places where he most needed " a sufficiency of local cur-

[1] Report of the Secretary of the Treasury, Dec. 6, 1815 ; State Papers, Finance, iii. 11.

rency for local purposes," Boston stood first; but he
borrowed in Boston less than one hundred thousand
dollars, and this only in Treasury notes. Next to
Boston stood New York; but in New York Dallas
borrowed only $658,000, also in Treasury notes. In
Philadelphia he obtained more than three millions,
and took $1,845,000 in the depreciated local cur-
rency. In Baltimore he took nearly two millions in
local currency; and in the bank paper of the District
of Columbia, which was the most depreciated of all,
he accepted $2,282,000 in local currency.[1] Thus the
loan which he had asked Congress to authorize for
the purpose of absorbing the excess of Treasury
notes, brought into the Treasury only about three
millions in these securities, while it relieved the
banks of Philadelphia, Baltimore, and Washington of
six millions of their depreciated paper, worth about
eighty cents in the dollar, and provided nothing to
redeem the government's overdue bills at Boston
and New York.

Had Dallas pursued a different course and funded
all the overdue Treasury notes at the market rate,
he might not have relieved New England, but he
would have placed the government in a position to
deal effectually with the suspended banks elsewhere.
The immediate result of his refusal to redeem the
dishonored Treasury notes was to depress their market value, and to discredit the government. Treasury
notes fell to eighty-eight and eighty-seven, while the

[1] Report of Dec. 6, 1815; State Papers, Finance, iii. 11.

six-per-cents fell as low as eighty-one. In Washington, Baltimore, and Philadelphia Dallas obtained enough local currency to meet local obligations, and doubtless saved to the government a small percentage by thus trafficking in its own discredit; but in gaining this advantage he offered encouragement to the over-issues of the suspended banks, and he helped to embarrass the solvent banks in the chief commercial centres as well as those in New England.[1]

At the close of the year 1815 the general effect of the peace was already well defined. The Southern States were in the full enjoyment of extraordinary prosperity. The Middle States were also prosperous and actively engaged in opening new sources of wealth. Only the Eastern States suffered under depression; but there it was so severe as to warrant a doubt whether New England could recover from the shock. The new epoch of American history began by the sudden decline of Massachusetts to the lowest point of relative prosperity and influence she had ever known, and by an equally sudden stimulus to the South and West. So discredited was Massachusetts that she scarcely ventured to complain, for every complaint uttered by her press was answered by the ironical advice that she should call another Hartford Convention.

[1] Gallatin to Jefferson, Nov. 27, 1815 ; Gallatin's writings, i. 666. Gallatin to Macon, April 23, 1816 ; Gallatin's writings, i. 697.

CHAPTER V.

BETWEEN 1801 and 1815, great changes in the American people struck the most superficial observer. The Rights of Man occupied public thoughts less, and the price of cotton more, in the later than in the earlier time. Although in 1815 Europe was suffering under a violent reaction against free government, Americans showed little interest and no alarm, compared with their emotions of twenty years before. Napoleon resumed his empire, and was overthrown at Waterloo, without causing the people of the United States to express a sign of concern in his fate; and France was occupied by foreign armies without rousing among Americans a fear of England. Foreign affairs seemed reduced to the question whether England would consent to negotiate a treaty of commerce.

After excluding most of the American demands, Lord Castlereagh consented to a commercial convention abolishing discriminating duties, and admitting American commerce with the East Indies. This treaty, signed July 3, seemed to satisfy American demands, and the British Ministry showed no wish to challenge new disputes. With France, the disturbed condition of government permitted no diplomatic arrangement. The only foreign country that required serious attention was Algiers ; and Decatur, with a strong squadron of the new American cruisers, speedily compelled the Dey to sign a treaty more favorable to the United States than he had yet signed with any other nation. Tunis and Tripoli showed a similar disposition, and Decatur returned home in the autumn, having settled to his satisfaction all the matters intrusted to his care.

Under such circumstances, without an anxiety in regard to foreign or domestic affairs, President Madison sent his Annual Message to Congress December 5, 1815. It told a pleasant story of successful administration and of rapidly growing income ; but its chief historical interest lay in the lines of future party politics that Madison more or less unconsciously sketched. The Message proved, or seemed to prove, that Madison's views and wishes lay in the direction of strong government. He advised " liberal provision " for defence ; more military academies ; an improved and enlarged navy ; effectual protection to manufactures ; new national roads and canals ; a national university ; and such an organization of the militia as would place it promptly and effectually under control of the national government. Madison seemed to take his stand, beyond further possibility of change, on the system of President Washington.

Dallas's report echoed the tone of Alexander Ham-

ilton. Very long, chiefly historical, and interesting
beyond the common, this Treasury Report of 1815
recommended a scale of annual expenditure exceeding twenty-seven millions, in place of the old scale of
ten millions. The expenditure was to be but a part
of the system. A protective tariff of customs duties
was assumed to be intended by Congress, and a national bank was urged as the only efficient means
by which the government could recover control over
the currency.

Although the President was less emphatic than
the secretary in holding a national bank to be the
only cure for the disorders of the currency, he was
prepared to go a step further by issuing government
paper as a national currency, and suggested that
alternative in his Message. A national bank or a
national currency was an equally energetic exercise
of supreme central powers not expressly granted by
the Constitution and much disputed by theorists.
Dallas's objection to the national currency did not
relate to its inefficiency, but to the practical difficulty
of issuing paper and keeping it in issue. Either
course of action implied a recurrence to the principles
of President Washington. The Executive proposed
to start afresh in 1816 from its point of departure
in 1790.

The Fourteenth Congress was well disposed to
support the attempt. Under the stress of war the
people had selected as their representatives the ablest
and most vigorous men of their generation. The

war leaders were mostly returned, — Calhoun, Clay, Lowndes, Richard M. Johnson, Peter B. Porter, and John Forsyth, — while the old peace party was strongly represented by Timothy Pickering, Daniel Webster, John Randolph, Grosvenor of New York, and Stanford of North Carolina; but perhaps the most distinguished member of all was William Pinkney of Maryland. A swarm of younger men, far above the average, reinforced both sides of the House. Philip P. Barbour sat again for Virginia. John McLean sat again for Ohio. Henry St. George Tucker came for the first time into the House. Joseph Hopkinson, Samuel D. Ingham, and John Sergeant raised the character of the Pennsylvania delegation; and Samuel Smith, at last ejected from the Senate by a Federalist legislature in Maryland, reappeared in the House for the first time since 1803.

The Senate was also improved. The disappearance of Leib and Samuel Smith was made more suggestive by the resignation of Giles. David Stone of North Carolina, another independent much given to opposition at critical moments, also resigned; and another of the same class, Joseph Anderson of Tennessee, who had been a member of the Senate since 1797, retired to become First Comptroller of the Treasury. These retirements removed the chief abettors of faction, and changed the character of the Senate until it seemed to belong to a different epoch. Jonathan Roberts still sat in the place of Leib. Armistead Mason took the seat of Giles, and with James Bar-

bour gave Madison for the first time the full sup-
port of Virginia.   Macon took the place of David
Stone.   George W. Campbell took the place of Joseph
Anderson.   Robert G. Harper, the old champion of
Federalism, succeeded Samuel Smith from Maryland.
The Senate scarcely recognized itself as the same
body that since 1808 had so persistently thwarted
and fretted the President.

In the arrangement of new party divisions the
Fourteenth Congress, unlike its recent predecessors,
consciously aimed to take a decided share.   The
House seemed for the first time in many years to
pride itself on intellectual superiority.   William Pinkney, Calhoun, Lowndes, Clay, Daniel Webster, John
Randolph, and their associates were not men who
bowed to authority, even of the people, but rather
looked on the task of government as a function of
superior intellect.   They proposed to correct what
they considered mistaken popular tendencies.   Each
expressed his ideas with sufficient clearness in the
form natural to him.   Calhoun generalized before
descending to particulars.[1]

" In the policy of nations," reasoned Calhoun, " there
are two extremes : one extreme, in which justice and
moderation may sink in feebleness ; another, in which
that lofty spirit which ought to animate all nations, particularly free ones, may mount up to military violence.
These extremes ought to be equally avoided ; but of the
two, I consider the first far the most dangerous. . . . I

[1] Speech of Jan. 31, 1816 ; Annals of Congress, 1815–1816,
p. 830.

consider the extreme of weakness not only the most dangerous of itself, but as that extreme to which the people of this country are peculiarly liable."

Clay, aiming at the same objects, dwelt chiefly on foreign dangers as the motive of the strong government he wished to establish. "That man must be blind to the indications of the future," he declared,[1] "who cannot see that we are destined to have war after war with Great Britain, until, if one of the two nations be not crushed, all grounds of collision shall have ceased between us." He wished to create a government that should control the destinies of both American continents by a display of armed force. "He confessed with infinite regret that he saw a supineness throughout the country which left him almost without hope that what he believed the correct policy would be pursued," toward aiding the Spanish colonies against their mother country. Both Calhoun and Clay admitted that they wished to govern in a sense not approved by an apparent majority of the nation; and the sympathies of the House were openly or secretly with them.

Of the contrary sentiment, John Randolph was the champion. Although his early career had ended in the most conspicuous failure yet known in American politics, he returned to the House, with intelligence morbidly sharpened, to begin a second epoch of his life with powers and materials that gave him

[1] Speech of Jan. 29, 1816; Annals of Congress, 1815–1816, p. 787.

the position of equal among men like Calhoun, Pinkney, and Webster. Randolph held a decisive advantage in wishing only to obstruct. He had no legislation to propose, and his political philosophy suited that extreme " to which," according to Calhoun, " the people of this country are peculiarly liable." Early in the session Randolph showed that he understood even better than Calhoun and Clay the division between himself and them. " If the warning voice of Patrick Henry," he said in the debate of January 31, 1816,[1] " had not apprised me long ago, the events of this day would have taught me that this Constitution does not comprise one people, but that there are two distinct characters in the people of this nation." In every growing people two or more distinct characters were likely to rise, else the people would not grow; but the primal character, which Randolph meant to represent, enjoyed the political advantage of passive resistance to impulse from every direction.

In reply to Calhoun, Randolph defined the issue with his usual skill of words : [2] —

" As the gentleman from South Carolina has presented the question to the House, they and the nation cannot have the slightest difficulty in deciding whether they will give up the States or not; whether they will, in fact, make this an elective monarchy. The question is whether or not we are willing to become one great consolidated

[1] Annals of Congress, 1815–1816, p. 841.
[2] Annals of Congress, 1815–1816, p. 844.

nation; or whether we have still respect enough for those old, respectable institutions to regard their integrity and preservation as a part of our policy."

Randolph's eccentricities, which amounted to insanity, prevented him from exercising in the House the influence to which his experience and abilities entitled him, but did not prevent him from reflecting the opinions of a large part of the nation, particularly in the South. Between these two impulses the Fourteenth Congress was to choose a path, subject to the future judgment of their constituents.

The Executive urged them on. Dallas began by sending to Calhoun, the chairman of the Committee on Currency, a plan for a national bank with a capital of thirty-five millions and power to increase it to fifty millions; with twenty-five directors, five of whom were to be appointed by the government to represent its share in the bank stock, of which the government was to subscribe one fifth.[1]

In another report, dated Feb. 12, 1816, Dallas recommended a protective tariff and sketched its details. Upon cotton fabrics he proposed a duty of thirty-three and one half per cent on their value; on woollens, twenty-eight per cent; on linen, hemp, and silk, twenty per cent; on paper, leather, etc., thirty-five per cent; on earthenware, glassware, etc., thirty per cent; on bar-iron, seventy-five cents per hundred weight; on rolled iron, a dollar and a half; and

[1] Dallas to Calhoun, Dec. 24, 1815; Annals of Congress, 1815–1816, p. 505.

on unenumerated articles, fifteen per cent. These
duties were avowedly protective, intended to serve
as the foundation of a system, and to perpetuate
the policy to which the Government stood pledged
by its legislation for the last six years. In connection with a proposed reduction of internal taxes, the
Bank and the Tariff covered the financial field.

The House first grappled with the subject of revenue. The Committee of Ways and Means, through
William Lowndes, reported, Jan. 9, 1816, a scheme
embodied in twelve Resolutions intended to serve as
the guide to definite legislation. Lowndes assumed a
net annual revenue of $25,369,000 ; and to obtain this
sum he proposed to shift the burden of about seven
million dollars from internal taxation to the customs,
by an addition of forty-two per cent to the rates of
permanent duty.[1] The direct tax was to be retained
to the amount of three million dollars, and an annual fund of $13,500,000 was to be set aside for
the interest and principal of the national debt.

Hardly had the debate begun when Randolph,
January 16, dragged the question of a protective
system into the prominence it was thenceforward to
maintain. Two years of repose had singularly improved his skill in the choice of language and in the
instigation of class against class.

"The manufacturer," said he,[2] "is the citizen of no
place or any place ; the agriculturist has his property, his

[1] Report of Committee ; Annals of Congress, 1815–1816, p. 516.
[2] Annals of Congress, 1815- 1816, p. 687.

lands, his all, his household Gods to defend, — and like that meek drudge the ox, who does the labor and ploughs the ground, then for his reward takes the refuse of the farm-yard, the blighted blades and the mouldy straw, and the mildewed shocks of corn for his support. . . . Alert, vigilant, enterprising, and active, the manufacturing interest are collected in masses, and ready to associate at a moments warning for any purpose of general interest to their body. Do but ring the fire-bell, and you can assemble all the manufacturing interest of Philadelphia in fifteen minutes. Nay, for the matter of that they are always assembled; they are always on the Rialto, and Shylock and Antonio meet there every day as friends, and compare notes, and possess in trick and intelligence what, in the goodness of God to them, the others can never possess."

Randolph's political sagacity was nowhere better shown than in replying, Jan. 31, 1816, to a speech of Calhoun : " On whom do your impost duties bear ?" he asked.[1]   " Upon whom bears the duty on coarse woollens and linens and blankets, upon salt, and all the necessaries of life ? On poor men, and on slaveholders." With a perception abnormally keen, Randolph fixed on the tariff and the slaveholders as the necessary combination to oppose the nationalizing efforts of Calhoun and Clay.

No leader of note supported Randolph. He stood alone, or with only the support of Stanford, as far as concerned debate ; but he led nearly half the House. Upon Benjamin Hardin's motion, February 3, to re-

[1] Annals of Congress, 1815–1816, p. 842.

peal the direct tax immediately and altogether, a motion which struck at the root of Dallas's scheme, the House decided by eighty-one votes against seventy-three to sustain the secretary. On the passage of the bill to continue the direct tax of three million dollars for one year, the minority lacked but a change of three votes to defeat it. The bill passed, March 4, by a vote of sixty-seven to sixty-three.

On the tariff the House was more closely divided. The Committee of Ways and Means consisted of seven members. Lowndes was chairman. Three other members were from the South, one of whom, Robertson of Louisiana, wished protection for sugar. Three members were from the North, one of whom, Ingham of Pennsylvania, represented Dallas's views. The chief question concerned the duty on cottons and woollens. So close was the division that Ingham, to use his own words, was struck dumb with astonishment when the committee, after adopting a duty of fifty-six per cent for the protection of sugar, voted to impose a duty of only twenty per cent on cottons and woollens. " It was, however, too glaringly inconsistent and palpably wrong to be persisted in, and therefore it was that the Committee of Ways and Means, upon reconsideration, substituted the twenty-five per cent which was reported in the bill." [1]

When the bill came before the House, Clay moved, March 21, to substitute the rate of thirty-three and

[1] Annals of Congress, 1815–1816, p. 1245.

one third per cent for that of twenty-five per cent on cottons, for the express purpose of testing the sense of the House. Clay and the Northern protectionists held that the committee's bill did not afford protection enough. The committee, also admitting the propriety of protection, maintained that twenty-five per cent was sufficient. On both sides some temper was shown, and charges of sectionalism were made. By a vote of sixty-eight to sixty-one, the House in committee voted, March 22, to impose a duty of thirty per cent. Daniel Webster then moved to limit this rate to two years, after which the duty should be twenty-five per cent for two years more, when it should be reduced to twenty per cent. Finally the House adopted a duty of twenty-five per cent for three years. Webster also carried, March 27, a motion to reduce the proposed duty on bar-iron from seventy-five to forty-five cents a hundred weight.

All the members of note, except Randolph, professed to favor protection. Calhoun was as decided as Ingham. " He believed the policy of the country required protection to our manufacturing establishments." [1] The bill was assumed to offer protection enough, and the House disputed only whether the adopted duties were or were not sufficient. The actual free-trade sentiment was shown, April 8, when Randolph made a final motion to postpone, and was beaten by a vote of ninety-five to forty-seven.

[1] Annals of Congress, 1815–1816, p. 1272.

The bill promptly passed the Senate, and was approved by the President April 27 ; but the true issue was undecided. No one could deny that if the duty of twenty-five per cent on cottons and woollens should prove to be insufficient, the House was pledged to increase it. The bill was avowedly protective. In regard to the coarser Indian cottons, it was practically prohibitive, since it valued them all, for tariff purposes, at twenty-five cents a yard, — a rate which on the cheaper fabrics raised the duty above one hundred per cent. Yet when the tariff of 1816 proved to be little protective, in after years it was commonly represented as a revenue and not a protective tariff. In substance, Randolph's opinions controlled the House.

Dallas was more fortunate in regard to the Bank. Randolph's hostility to State banks was greater than to the Bank of the United States. Calhoun reported, January 8, the bill to incorporate for twenty years a new National Bank with a capital of thirty-five million dollars, and supported it, February 26, by a speech showing that the Bank was a proper means for attaining the Constitutional object of restoring the money of the country to its true medium. Active opposition came chiefly from the Federalists. Even Samuel Smith seemed to plead rather that the State banks should be gently treated than that the National Bank should be opposed. Randolph, while professing hostility to the new Bank on any and every ground suggested by others, concluded by pledging himself to support any adequate means for reducing the over-powering influence of the State banks. Clay thought himself obliged to leave the Speaker's chair in order to recant in the most public manner his errors of 1811. Forsyth, one of Calhoun's ablest allies, went so far in his support of the measure as to assert without reserve that the power to suspend specie pay-ments — a power expressly reserved to the govern-ment by Calhoun's bill — belonged undoubtedly to Congress, an opinion which the House did not share. In the Republican ranks open opposition to the Bank seemed almost silenced; and the member who made himself most conspicuous in hostility to the bill was Daniel Webster, — the last of all in whom such a course was natural.

Webster's criticism on Calhoun's Constitutional ar-gument was made in his loftiest manner. The cur-rency, he said, needed no reform, for it was, by the Constitution and the law, gold and silver; nor had Congress the right to make any other medium cur-rent. The true remedy was for Congress to inter-dict the bills of the suspended banks.[1] Had he been content to rest his opposition on that ground alone, Webster could not have been answered, although he might have been regarded as an impracticable politi-cian; but as the bill came toward its passage, and as several Federalists declared in its favor, he pressed his hostility so far, and with so much dogmatism, that several of his own party revolted, and Grosvenor of

[1] Annals of Congress, 1815–1816, p. 1091.

New York replied sharply that he did not propose to be drilled to vote on whatever any one might choose to call a principle.

In spite of determined opposition from Webster, Pitkin, John Sergeant, and other Federalists, the House passed the bill, March 14, by a vote of eighty to seventy-one. The majority was small, but of the minority not less than thirty-eight were Federalists; and, omitting Randolph and Stanford, only thirty-one Republicans voted against the bill. The House contained one hundred and seventeen Republicans. In the Senate the opposition was almost wholly confined to Federalists, and the bill passed by a majority much larger than that in the House. Twenty-two senators voted in its favor; only twelve voted against it, and of the twelve only four were Republicans. The President approved it April 10; and thus, after five years of financial disorder, the Republican party reverted to the system of Washington, and resumed powers it had found indispensable to government.

The Federalists of New England were in a situation too alarming to bear even the little delay required to organize the Bank. For them a general return to specie payments was the only escape from imminent ruin; and acting on this conviction, Webster moved, April 26, a joint Resolution ordering that all taxes should be collected after Feb. 1, 1817, in some medium equivalent to specie, thus allowing but nine months for the work of resumption. The same day the House passed the Resolution by the decisive majority of seventy-one to thirty-four. The Senate substituted February 20 as the day of resumption, and passed the Resolution April 29, which was approved by the President the next day.

In contrast with the imbecility of many previous Congresses, the vigor of the Fourteenth Congress in thus settling the new scale of government was remarkable; but other measures of importance were not wanting. An Act approved April 29 appropriated one million dollars annually for three years to build ships of war; an Act approved April 19 authorized the people of Indiana to form a State government. A bill, which passed the House but was postponed by the Senate and became law at the next session, provided for the admission of Mississippi. In still another direction the House showed its self-confidence in a manner that caused unusual popular excitement. It undertook to increase the pay of its own members and of senators.

The scale of salary for public officials was low. The President, relatively highly paid, received twenty-five thousand dollars. The Secretaries of State and Treasury received five thousand; those of War and Navy, four thousand; the Attorney-General, three thousand; Chief-Justice Marshall was paid four thousand, and the six associate justices received thirty-five hundred dollars each.

While the Executive and Judiciary were paid regular salaries, Congress stood on a different footing. Legislators had never been paid what was considered an equivalent for their time and services. They were supposed to be unpaid; but such a rule excluded poor men from the public service, and therefore the colonial legislatures adopted a practice, which Congress continued, of allowing what were supposed to be the reasonable expenses of members. The First Congress fixed upon six dollars a day, and six dollars for every twenty miles of estimated journey, as a suitable scale of expense both for senators and representatives;[1] and the same rate had been continued for twenty-five years. No one supposed it sufficient to support a household, but poor men could live upon it. Desha of Kentucky averred that it was a fair allowance for the average representative. According to him, board was twelve or thirteen dollars a week, and the total cost of a session of one hundred and fifty days amounted to five hundred and seventy or eighty dollars; so that the western and southwestern members, with whose habits he was familiar, carried home, with their mileage, about four hundred and fifty dollars in savings.[2]

In the pride of conscious superiority the Fourteenth Congress undertook to change the system; and Richard M. Johnson, probably the most popular member of the House, assumed the risk of popular displeasure. In moving for a committee, March 4, Johnson repudiated the idea of increasing the pay; and his committee, including Webster, Pitkin, Jackson, the

[1] Act of Sept. 22, 1789. Act of March 10, 1796.
[2] Annals of Congress; 1816–1817, p. 492.

President's brother-in-law, Grosvenor, and McLean of Ohio, reported through him that fifteen hundred dollars a year was the correct equivalent of six dollars a day.

The bill known as the Compensation Bill was reported March 6, and was debated for two days with some animation. Among its supporters John Randolph was prominent, and gave offence to the opponents of the measure by his usual tactics. Most of the friends of the bill stoutly insisted that it did not increase the pay ; most of its opponents averred that it more than doubled the amount. Calhoun admitted the increase of pay, and favored it, in order to retain " young men of genius without property " in the public service. The bill was hurried through the House.

" The Compensation Bill," said Forsyth at the next session,[1] " was the only one of any interest pushed through the Committee of the whole House and ordered to a third reading in a single day. All motions to amend were rejected ; for the committee to rise and report progress and ask leave to sit again, met with a similar fate. . . . The House refused repeated propositions to adjourn, and continued its sittings until the bill was ordered to be engrossed."

No time was lost. Johnson moved for a committee March 4 ; the committee reported the bill March 6 ; the House in committee took it up March 7, and reported it the same day. The House passed it March

[1] Annals of Congress ; 1816–1817, p. 559.

8, by a vote of eighty-one to sixty-seven.   In the
Senate the bill was read for a second time March 12.
In the course of the debate one of the New Jersey
senators, commenting on the haste shown by the
House to pass the bill, added that also " in the Senate postponement, commitment, and amendment are
all refused, and it is to be pushed through by main
strength with a haste altogether unusual."   The
Senate passed it March 14, by a vote of twenty-one
to eleven ; and it received the President's signature
March 19, barely a fortnight after Johnson's request
for a committee.

   At the time when the bill was still under consideration by the President, and the House had just
passed the Bank Act, the Republican members of
both Houses met to nominate a candidate to succeed
Madison as President.   Three candidates were in the
field, — Daniel D. Tompkins, William H. Crawford,
and James Monroe.

   The choice was a matter of small consequence, for
any candidate of the Republican party was sure of
almost unanimous election, and all were respectable
men ; but Tompkins could expect little support at a
time when Congress selected the candidate, for only
men well known in the national service were likely
to satisfy the standard of Congressmen.   The true
contest lay between Crawford and Monroe, and was
complicated, as far as the candidates themselves
understood it, by personal intrigues on both sides.
Perhaps Crawford's strength was the greater, for four

fifths of the New York members favored him rather than the Virginian.[1] In cases where no strong feeling fixed results, dexterity in management might overcome a preference between persons; and by some means never explained, the preference of the New York members for Crawford was overcome. One of these members — a competent observer — believed that Martin Van Buren and Peter B. Porter, for reasons of their own, prevented New York from declaring for Crawford when such a declaration would have decided the result.[2] Crawford himself at the last professed to withdraw from the contest,[3] and several of his warm friends did not attend the caucus. On the evening of March 15, one hundred and nineteen senators and representatives appeared in the hall of the House of Representatives in obedience to an anonymous notice addressed to one hundred and forty-three Republican members. Sixty-five, or less than half the Republican representation, voted for Monroe; fifty-four voted for Crawford; and eighty-five then united in nominating Governor Tompkins as Vice-President.

Monroe's character was well known, and his elevation to the Presidency was a result neither of great popularity nor of exceptional force, but was rather due to the sudden peace which left him the residuum of Madison's many Cabinets. A long list of resig-

[1] Hammond's New York, i. 409.

[2] Hammond's New York, i. 409.

[3] Crawford to Gallatin, May 10, 1816; Gallatin's Writings, i. 702.

nations alone remained to recall the memory of his
associates. Robert Smith, Cæsar Rodney, William
Eustis, Paul Hamilton, Gallatin, G. W. Campbell,
William Jones, William Pinkney, and John Armstrong had all resigned in succession, leaving Monroe
and Dallas in possession of the government when
peace was declared. Dallas was not a popular character, whatever were his abilities or services; and no
other man occupied high ground. Under such circumstances the strength shown by Crawford was
surprising, and proved that Monroe, notwithstanding his advantages, was regarded with no exclusive
favor.

In truth Monroe had no party. His original
friends were the old Republicans, — John Taylor of
Caroline, Littleton Tazewell, John Randolph, and
their associates, from whom he had drawn apart.
His new friends were chiefly northern Democrats,
whose motives for preferring him to Crawford were
selfish. In any case an epoch of personal politics
could be foreseen, for men like Crawford, Calhoun,
and Clay never submitted long to a superior ; and
for such an epoch Monroe was probably the best
choice.

Shortly after the nomination Dallas gave notice to
the President that he meant to retire from the Treasury in order to resume his practice at the bar.[1]
Madison immediately wrote to Gallatin, April 12,
inviting him to resume charge of the Treasury ; but

[1] Life and Writings of A. J. Dallas, p. 139.

Gallatin was weary of domestic politics, and preferred diplomacy. He went as minister to France, while Dallas remained at the Treasury until October, to set the new Bank in motion.

These arrangements closed the first session of the Fourteenth Congress, which adjourned April 30, leaving Madison in unaccustomed peace, harassed by no more enemies or dissensions, to wait the close of his public life.

CHAPTER VI.

THE prosperity that followed the Peace of Ghent suffered no check during the year 1816, or during the remainder of Madison's term. The exports of domestic produce, officially valued at $45,000,000 for the year ending Sept. 30, 1815, were valued at nearly $65,000,000 for the following year, and exceeded $68,000,000 for 1817. The Southern States still supplied two thirds of the exported produce. Cotton to the amount of $24,000,000, tobacco valued at nearly $13,000,000, and rice at $3,500,000, contributed more than forty of the sixty-five millions of domestic exports in 1816. The tables [1] showed that while South Carolina, Georgia, and Louisiana gained with unparalleled rapidity, New England lost ground, and New York only maintained its uniform movement. While the domestic exports of Georgia and Louisiana trebled in value, those of New York increased from eight to fourteen millions.

Notwithstanding the great importations from Europe which under ordinary conditions would have counterbalanced the exports, the exchanges soon turned in favor of the United States. Before the close of 1816

[1] State Papers ; Commerce and Navigation, i. 929.

specie in considerable quantities began to flow into the country. Canada, being nearest, felt the drain first, and suffered much inconvenience from it; but during the summer of 1816 and 1817 Europe also shipped much specie to America. Every ship brought some amount, until the export began to affect the Bank of England, which at last found its bullion diminishing with alarming rapidity. The returns showed a drain beginning in July or August, 1817, when the Bank of England held £11,668,000, until August, 1819, when the supply was reduced to £3,595,000; and in the interval a commercial crisis, with a general destruction of credit, occurred. The reaction could not fail in the end to affect America as it affected England, but the first result was stimulating beyond all previous experience. In England the drain of specie embarrassed government in returning to specie payments. In the United States the influx of specie made the return easy, if not necessary.

The recovery of internal exchanges kept pace with the influx of specie. At Boston, July 27, 1816, United States six-per-cent bonds were quoted at eighty-five, and Treasury notes at ninety-four to ninety-four and one-half; at New York six-per-cents stood at ninety, and Treasury notes at par; in Philadelphia six-per-cents were worth ninety-eight, and Treasury notes one hundred and seven; in Baltimore six-per-cents were selling at one hundred and two, and Treasury notes at one hundred and twelve.

During the next five months the recovery was steady and rapid. The banks of New York, September 26, began to cash their one-dollar notes, thus relieving the community from the annoyance of fractional currency. October 26 the six-per-cents stood at ninety-two in Boston, at ninety-three and one-half in New York, at ninety-eight in Philadelphia, and at one hundred and one and one-half in Baltimore. November 28 they sold at ninety-six in Boston; November 30 they sold at ninety-six and one-quarter in New York, at one hundred and one and one-half in Philadelphia, and at one hundred and five in Baltimore. January 1, 1817, the Treasury resumed payments at Boston in Boston money, and no further discredit attached to government securities.

The banks of the Middle States were less disposed than the government to hasten the return of specie payments. In order to do so, they were obliged to contract their circulation and discounts to an extent that would have been unendurable in any time but one of great prosperity; and only the threats of Dallas overcame their reluctance, even under most favorable conditions. Both Dallas and the President were irritated by their slowness.[1] July 22, 1816, the Secretary of the Treasury issued a circular warning them that, at whatever cost, the Treasury must carry into effect the order of Congress to collect the revenue, after Feb. 20, 1817, only in specie or its equivalent. "The banks in the States to the South," he

[1] Madison to Dallas, July 16, 1816; Life of A. J. Dallas, p. 453.

said,[1] " and to the west of Maryland, are ready and willing, it is believed, to co-operate in the same measure. The objection, or the obstacle to the measure, principally rests with the banks of the Middle States." Dallas invited them to assist the Treasury in resuming specie payments with the least possible delay; and accordingly the banks of the Middle States held a convention at Philadelphia, August 6, to consider their course.

This convention, on discussing the possibility of resumption, agreed that the banks needed more time than the government was disposed to allow. Credit had been necessarily expanded by the unusual scale of commerce and enterprise. So sudden and violent a contraction as was required for specie payments could not fail to distress the public, and might cause great suffering. Yet in some degree the new United States Bank could relieve this pressure; and therefore the resumption should not be attempted by the State banks until the National Bank should be fairly opened and ready to begin its discounts. The State banks in convention foresaw, or imagined, that the United States Bank could not begin operations so early as Feb. 20, 1817, and they declined to risk resumption without its aid. Acting on this impression, they met Dallas's urgency by a formal recommendation that their banks should begin to pay specie, not on the 20th of February, but on the first Monday of July, 1817.

[1] Niles, x. 376.

This decision, though unsatisfactory to Dallas and the President, could not be considered unreasonable. Credit was expanded beyond the limit of safety, and the government was largely responsible for the expansion. Many of the State banks were probably unsound from the first, and needed careful management. Between 1810 and 1830, on a total capital of one hundred and forty millions, the bank failures amounted to thirty millions, or more than one fifth of the whole.[1] In Pennsylvania the country banks reduced their issues from $4,756,000 in November, 1816, to $1,318,000 in November, 1819. The latter moment was one of extreme depression, but the former was probably not that of the greatest expansion. When the banks of the Middle States held their convention, Aug. 6, 1816, contraction had already begun, and steadily continued, while specie flowed into the country to supply a foundation for bank paper. Under such circumstances the banks asked no extravagant favor in recommending that eleven months, instead of seven, should be allowed for resumption.

Dallas was not disposed to concede this favor. Having at last the necessary machinery for controlling the State banks, he used it with the same vigor that marked all his acts. No sooner had the convention announced its unwillingness to co-operate with the Treasury in executing the order of Congress, than Dallas issued instructions, August 16,[2]

---

[1] Gallatin, Banks and Currency ; Works, iii. 293.

[2] Niles, x. 423.

hastening the preparations for opening the National Bank as early as Jan. 1, 1817. Soon afterward, September 12, he renewed his notice that the notes of suspended banks would be rejected by the Treasury after Feb. 20, 1817.

The Bank subscription was filled in August, a deficit of three million dollars being taken by Stephen Girard in a single mass.[1] In October the board of directors was chosen by the shareholders, and in November the directors met and elected as President the former Secretary of the Navy, William Jones. One of their first acts was much debated, and was strongly opposed in the board of directors by J. J. Astor. They sent John Sergeant, of Philadelphia, abroad with authority to purchase some millions of bullion; and his mission was calculated to impress on the public the conviction that specie payments were to be resumed as soon as the Bank could open its doors.

Hurried by Dallas, the Bank actually began its operations in January, 1817, and under the double pressure from the Treasury the State banks had no choice but to yield. Another meeting was held at Philadelphia, February 1, consisting of delegates from the banks of New York, Philadelphia, Baltimore, and Richmond. The convention entered into a compact with the Secretary of the Treasury to resume payments, on certain conditions, at the day fixed by Congress. The compact was carried into effect

[1] Dallas to Madison, Aug. 27, 1816 ; Life of Dallas, p. 471.

February 20, a few days before the close of Madison's Presidency. Its success was magical. In New York, at ten o'clock on the morning of February 20, specie was at two and one half per cent premium. The banks opened their doors, and in half an hour all was once more regular and normal.

Thus the worst financial evil of the war was removed within two years after the proclamation of peace. A debt of about one hundred and thirty millions remained; but the people which only twenty years before had shrunk with fear and disgust from a debt of eighty millions, gave scarcely a thought in 1816 to their funded obligations. The difference between the two periods was not so much economical as political. Population and wealth had increased, but the experience of the people had advanced more rapidly than their numbers or capital. In measuring the political movement shrewd judges might easily err, for the elections of 1816 showed little apparent change in parties; but in truth parties had outgrown their principles, and in politics, as in finance, the close of Madison's Administration obliterated old distinctions.

Neither party admitted the abandonment of its dogmas. The New York election in the spring of 1816 showed no considerable change in votes. In 1810 Governor Tompkins was elected by ten thousand majority; even in the dark days of 1813 he had a majority of thirty-six hundred; in 1816, notwithstanding his popularity and the success of his war administration, his majority was less than seven thousand. In Massachusetts John Brooks, who succeeded Governor Strong as candidate of the Federalist party, received forty-nine thousand five hundred votes, while Samuel Dexter received forty-seven thousand four hundred. Six years before, in 1810, the Republican candidate, Elbridge Gerry, had received more than forty-six thousand five hundred, and Governor Strong had polled only forty-four thousand. Apparently the Republicans had lost ground in Massachusetts since 1810. In Connecticut, where the election turned on church issues, the result was somewhat different. The Anglican church, a small body but rich and influential, strongly Federalist in politics and conservative in character, joined the Democrats to overthrow the reign of the Congregational clergy. Oliver Wolcott, a Federalist who supported the war, was their candidate; and the combination nearly carried the State. Wolcott received about ten thousand two hundred votes; his Federalist opponent was elected by eleven thousand three hundred and seventy votes. The Federalists also carried Rhode Island, once a strongly Democratic State, and seemed socially as well as politically to be little affected by their many mistakes and misfortunes.

Yet every one felt that real distinctions of party no longer existed. The Anglicans of Connecticut, the Unitarians of Boston, the Universalists and Baptists, looked chiefly to the overthrow of the established New England church; and the Democrats of New York, like the Republicans of Virginia and North Carolina, labored for a system of internal improvements and for increased energy in national government.   Parties, no longer held together by discipline, were liable at any moment to fall into confusion ; and, as frequently happened in such stages of public opinion, they were extraordinarily affected by influences seemingly trivial.   In 1816 the relaxation of party spirit resulted in a phenomenon never before witnessed. The whole community rose against its own representatives, and showed evident pleasure in condemning them.   The occasion for this outbreak of popular temper was the Compensation Bill ; but the instinct that could alone account for the public pleasure in punishing public men, could not be explained by a cause so trifling as that Act.

At the next session of Congress, Calhoun, lapsing in the middle of a speech into his usual meditative speculation, remarked, as though he were perplexed to account for his own theory, that in his belief the House of Representatives was not a favorite with the American people.[1]   Had he expressed the opinion that freedom of thought or speech was not a favorite with the American people, he would have said nothing more surprising.   If the House was not a favorite, what part of the government was popular, and what could be hoped for representative government itself ?   Of all the machinery created by the Constitution, the House alone directly reflected and

[1] Annals of Congress, 1816–1817, pp. 392, 505, 604.

represented the people ; and if the people disliked it, they disliked themselves.

The people best knew whether Calhoun was right. Certainly the House, owing in part to its size, its frequent elections and changes, its lack of responsibility and of social unity, was the least steady and least efficient branch of government. Readers who have followed the history here closed, have been surprised at the frequency with which the word *imbecility* has risen in their minds in reading the proceedings of the House. So strong was the same impression at the time, that in the year 1814, at the close of the war, every earnest patriot in the Union, and many men who were neither earnest nor patriotic, were actively reproaching the House for its final failure, at an apparent crisis of the national existence, to call out or organize any considerable part of the national energies. The people in truth, however jealous of power, would have liked in imagination, though they would not bear in practice, to be represented by something nobler, wiser, and purer than their own average honor, wisdom, and purity. They could not make an ideal of weakness, ignorance, or vice, even their own ; and as they required in their religion the idea of an infinitely wise and powerful deity, they revolted in their politics from whatever struck them as sordid or selfish. The House reflected their own weaknesses ; and the Compensation Act seemed to them an expression of their own least agreeable traits. They rebelled against a petty appropriation of money,

after enduring for years a constant succession of
worse offences.

" Who would have believed," asked John Randolph,[1]
six months afterward, — " who would have believed," he
repeated, " that the people of the United States would
have borne all the privations and losses of the late war,
and of the measures that led to it; that they would have
quietly regarded a national debt, swelled to an amount
unknown, — to an amount greater than the whole expense of our seven years' war; that they would have
seen the election of President taken out of their hands
[by the caucus]; that they would have borne with abuse
and peculation through every department of the government, — and that the great Leviathan, which slept
under all these grievances, should be roused into action
by the Fifteen-Hundred-Dollar Law?"

Only with difficulty could members persuade themselves that the public anger was real. They could
not at first conceive that the people should be seriously angry because Congress had thought proper to
pay its members a sum not in itself extravagant or
adequate to their services. Not until the members
returned to their homes did they appreciate the force
of public feeling; but they soon felt themselves helpless to resist it. Richard M. Johnson and Henry
Clay, the two most popular men in Kentucky, found
their entire constituency attacking them. " When I
went home," said Clay,[2] " I do not recollect to have

[1] Annals of Congress, 1816–1817, p. 501.
[2] Annals of Congress, 1816–1817, p. 497.

met with one solitary individual of any description
of party who was not opposed to the Act, — who did
not, on some ground or other, think it an improper
and unjust law." Benjamin Hardin,[1] another of the
Kentucky victims, said : " If a man came into the
county court to be appointed a constable or surveyor
of the road, he entered his solemn protest against the
Compensation Law. If a petty demagogue wanted to
get into the legislature, he must post up, or put in the
newspapers, his protest against it."

" There was at first a violent excitement," said Philip
P. Barbour of Virginia ;[2] "gentlemen might call it, if
they pleased, a storm. But that storm, even when its
fury abated, subsided into a fixed and settled discontent
at the measure ; it met the disapprobation and excited
the discontent of the grave, the reflecting, and the deliberate ; and such he believed to be the case with an immense
majority of the American people."

Grand juries denounced it in Vermont and Georgia ;
the State legislature denounced it in Massachusetts ;
town-meetings protested against it ; county conven-
tions sat upon it ; all classes and parties united in
condemning it, and the brunt of this sweeping popular reproval fell upon the House of Representatives.
Close as the House stood to the people, its want of
popularity was evident, — as Calhoun, with his usual
insight, bore witness. The House had as a body
few friends and no protection against popular tem-

[1] Annals of Congress, 1816–1817, p. 535.
[2] Annals of Congress, 1816–1817, p. 517.

pests. The first to suffer, it was always the last to escape. One after another the weaker members gave way, and either declined re-election or were not re-elected. The chiefs succeeded for the most part by personal popularity in maintaining their hold on their districts, although several leading members lost their seats.

Even against so feeble and factious a body as the Thirteenth Congress, such condemnation would have seemed exceptional; but the peculiarity that made this popular reproof singular and suggestive was the popular admission that the Fourteenth Congress, for ability, energy, and usefulness, never had a superior, and perhaps, since the First Congress, never an equal. Such abilities were uncommon in any legislative body, American or European. Since Federalist times no Congress had felt such a sense of its own strength, and such pride in its own superiority; none had filled so fully the popular ideal of what the people's representatives should be. That this remarkable body of men should have incurred almost instantly the severest popular rebuke ever visited on a House of Representatives, could not have been mere accident.

The politics of 1816 seemed absorbed in the Compensation Act, and in the union of parties to condemn their representatives. The Senate escaped serious censure; and President Madison, so far from being called to account for errors real or imaginary, seemed to enjoy popularity never before granted to any President at the expiration of his term. The apparent

contentment was certainly not due to want of grievances. The internal taxes pressed hard on the people, especially in New England, where the suffering
was general and in some places severe; but no popular cry for reduction of taxes disturbed the elections.
No portion of the country seemed displeased that a
fourth Virginian should be made President by the
intrigues of a Congressional caucus. The State legislatures for the most part chose as usual the Presidential electors; and in December the public learned,
almost without interest, that James Monroe had received one hundred and eighty-three electoral votes,
representing sixteen States, while Rufus King had
received thirty-four electoral votes, representing Massachusetts, Connecticut, and Delaware. Daniel D.
Tompkins of New York was made Vice-President by
the same process. Nothing in the elections, either
for President or for Congress, showed that the people were disposed to scrutinize sharply the workings
of any part of their government except the House of
Representatives.

As the winter approached when Madison was to
meet Congress for the last time, the sixteen years of
his official service, which had been filled with excitement and violence, were ending in political stagnation.
Party divisions had so nearly disappeared that nothing prevented the President elect from selecting as the
head of his Cabinet the son of the last Federalist President, who had been the object of more violent attack
from the Republican party than had been directed

against any other Federalist. Old Republicans, like
Macon and John Randolph, were at loss to know
whether James Monroe or J. Q. Adams had departed
farthest from their original starting-points. At times
they charged one, at times the other, with desertion
of principle; but on the whole their acts tended to
betray a conviction that J. Q. Adams was still a Federalist in essentials, while Monroe had ceased to be
an old Republican. In the political situation of 1817,
if Jefferson and his contemporaries were right in
their estimates, Federalist views of government were
tending to prevail over the views of the Jeffersonian party.

With this tendency, the national prosperity and the
state of the Treasury had much to do. Dallas carried
out his purpose, and in October quitted the Treasury.
In retiring, he left with the President a sketch of the
condition of the finances such as no previous secretary had been so fortunate as to present. For the
year ending Sept. 30, 1816, the receipts amounted to
$47,670,000.[1] From the customs, which Dallas had
estimated at $21,000,000, duties to the amount of
$36,000,000 were received. A surplus of more than
$20,000,000 was likely to accumulate in the Treasury
before the close of the year.

Old ideas of economy and strict restraints on expenditure could not long maintain themselves in the
presence of such an income; but besides the tempta-
tion to expand the sphere of government in expen-

[1] Statement, etc. ; State Papers, Finances, iii. 487.

ditures, other influences were at work to establish
Federalist principles in the system itself. Dallas remained in office chiefly in order to organize the Bank,
and to render certain the resumption of specie payments. When he retired, in October, 1816, both
objects were practically attained. His administration of the Treasury had then lasted two years. He
found the government bankrupt; he left it with a
surplus of twenty millions for the year. His measures not only relieved the country from financial disorders equalled only by those of the Revolutionary
War, but also fixed the financial system in a firm
groove for twenty years. He failed only in his attempt to obtain from Congress a larger degree of protection for domestic industries. Had his scheme of
protection been adopted, possibly the violence of subsequent changes in revenue and legislation might
have been moderated, and certainly the result could
have been no more mischievous than it was.

Dallas retired to private life by his own wish, and
the public three months afterward heard with surprise and regret the news of his sudden death. Like
most of the men who rendered decisive services during the war, he received no public reward commen-
surate with his deserts. He fared better than
Armstrong, who created the army; but even Gallatin, who shaped the diplomatic result, was content
to retire into the comparative obscurity of the mission
to Paris; while Perry and Macdonough, whose personal qualities had decided the fortunes of two cam-

paigns and won the military basis on which peace
could be negotiated, received no more reward than
fell to the lot of third-rate men. In the case of Dallas and Gallatin, the apparent neglect was their own
choice. Gallatin might have returned to the Treasury, but declined it ; and the President transferred
W. H. Crawford from the War Department to the
charge of the finances, while Clay was offered the
War Department in succession to Crawford.

These arrangements affected Madison but little.
He had no longer an object to gain from the dis-
posal of patronage, and he sought to smooth the
path of his successor rather than to benefit himself. Few Presidents ever quitted office under circumstances so agreeable as those which surrounded
Madison. During the last two years of his Administration almost every month brought some difficulty
to an end, or accomplished some long-desired result.
The restoration of the finances was perhaps his greatest source of satisfaction ; but the steadiness with
which the whole country, except New England, recovered prosperity and contentment afforded him a
wider and more constant pleasure. The ravages of
war left few traces. Even at Washington the new
public buildings were pressed forward so rapidly that
the effects of fire were no longer seen. The Capitol
began to rise from its ruins. The new halls of Congress promised to do honor to Madison's judgment.
Benjamin Latrobe was the architect in charge ; and
his Representative Chamber, without reproducing that

which Jefferson had helped to design, was dignified and worthy of its object. The old sandstone columns were replaced by another material. On the shore of the Potomac, near Leesburg, Latrobe noticed a conglomerate rock, containing rounded pebbles of various sizes and colors, and capable of being worked in large masses. His love of novelty led him to employ this conglomerate as an ornamental stone for the columns of the Hall of Representatives; and the effect was not without elegance.

Several years were still to pass before Congress occupied its permanent quarters, and Madison did not return to the White House; but the traces of national disaster disappeared in the process of reconstruction before he quitted the Presidency.

Surrounded by these pleasant conditions, Madison saw Congress assemble for the last time to listen to his requests. The Message which he sent to the legislature December 3 showed the extinction of party issues, and suggested no action that seemed likely to revive party disputes in any new form. The President expressed regret at the depression in shipping and manufactures, the branches of industry unfavorably affected by the peace. He suggested that Congress should consider especially the need of laws counteracting the exclusive navigation system of Great Britain. He recommended once more the time-worn subjects of the Militia and a National University. He asked for legislation against the Slave Trade, and urged a re-modification of the Judiciary.

He requested Congress to create a new Executive
department for Home or Interior Affairs, and to
place the Attorney-General's office on the footing of
a department. He gave a flattering account of the
finances ; and his Message closed with a panegyric
on the people and their government, for seeking " by
appeals to reason, and by its liberal examples, to in-
fuse into the law which governs the civilized world a
spirit which may diminish the frequency or circum-
scribe the calamities of war, and meliorate the social
and beneficent relations of peace : a government, in
a word, whose conduct, within and without, may
bespeak the most noble of all ambitions, — that of
promoting peace on earth and good-will to man."

For the moment, Congressmen were too much interested in their own quarrel to sympathize strongly
with panegyrics on the people or their government.
The members of the House returned to Washington
mortified, angry, and defiant, disgusted alike with the
public and with the public service. No sooner were
the standing committees announced, December 4,
than Richard M. Johnson moved for a special committee on the repeal of the Compensation Law, and
supported his motion in an unusually elaborate speech,
filled with argument, complaint, and irritation. The
committee was appointed, — Johnson at its head ;
William Findley of Pennsylvania, second ; Daniel
Webster, third, with four other members. After
twelve days' consideration, December 18, the committee presented a report, written by Webster, defend-

ing the Act, but recommending a return to the *per diem* system, in deference to the popular wish. The scale of the new allowance was left for Congress to determine.

Until this personal quarrel was discussed, no other business received attention. The debate — postponed till Jan. 14, 1817, to save the dignity of the House — lasted, to the exclusion of other business, until January 23. As an exhibition of personal and corporate character, it was entertaining; but it contained little of permanent interest or value. Calhoun, always above his subject, spoke with much force against yielding to popular outcry. "This House," he said, "is the foundation of the fabric of our liberty. So happy is its constitution, that in all instances of a general nature its duty and its interests are inseparable. If he understood correctly the structure of our government, the prevailing principle is not so much a balance of power, as a well-connected chain of responsibility. That responsibility commenced here, and this House is the centre of its operation." The idea that the people had "resolved the government into its original elements, and resumed to themselves their primitive power of legislation," was inconsistent with the idea that responsibility commenced and centred in the House. "Are we bound in all cases to do what is popular?" asked Calhoun. Could the House shift responsibility from itself to the people without destroying the foundation of the entire fabric?

Like most of Calhoun's speculations, this question could receive its answer only in some distant future. The Compensation Law lowered permanently the self-respect of the House, which had already declined from the formation of the government. " Of that House," said Richard Henry Wilde of Georgia,[1] " he feared it might be said in the words of Claudian : ' A fronte recedant imperii.' Yes, sir, they were receding, — they had receded from the front of empire. That House, formerly the favorite of the American nation, the first and most important branch of the government, the immediate image of the people, had been losing, and continued to lose, — certainly by no fault of theirs, but by the working of causes not for him to develop, — that rank and power in the government originally belonging to them, and which others at their expense had been secretly acquiring." Yet the House, while repealing the law, refused to admit itself in the wrong. The law was repealed only so far as it applied to subsequent Congresses. Leaving its successors to fix whatever compensation they thought proper for their services, the Fourteenth Congress adhered to its own scale, and took the money it was expected to refund.

Having disposed of this personal affair, the House turned to serious business, and completed its remarkable career by enacting several measures of far-reaching importance.

The first of these measures was a Navigation Act,

[1] Annals of Congress, 1816–1817, p. 604.

approved March 1, 1817, imposing on foreign vessels the same restrictions and prohibitions which were imposed by foreign nations on Americans. The second resembled the first in its object, but related only to the importation of plaster of Paris from Nova Scotia and New Brunswick. These two Acts began a struggle against the foreign navigation systems, which ended in their overthrow.

For the present the House postponed the establishment of an Interior Department, and allowed the Attorney-General to remain without an office or a clerk; but it passed an Act, approved March 3, 1817, concentrating in the Treasury the accounting business of government, and appointing four more auditors and one more comptroller for the purpose.

The fourth and most important measure that became law was a Neutrality Act, approved March 3, 1817, which authorized collectors of customs to seize and detain "any vessel manifestly built for warlike purposes, . . . when the number of men shipped on board, or other circumstances, shall render it probable that such vessel is intended by the owner" to cruise against the commerce of a friendly State. Nearly fifty years were to pass before the people of the United States learned to realize the full importance of this Act, which laid the foundation for all the subsequent measures taken by the United States and Great Britain for preserving neutrality in their relations with warring countries.[1] The Neu-

[1] Dana's Wheaton, pp. 541–542, *note.*

trality Act of 1817 furnished the measure of neutral obligations.

Besides these important laws, the Fourteenth Congress passed another bill, which closed its own activity and that of President Madison. None of the previous measures bore any direct relation to party politics, either past or future; but the bill for internal improvements, which Congress passed and the President vetoed, was an event of no small meaning in party history.

Calhoun moved, December 16, "that a committee be appointed to inquire into the expediency of setting apart . . . a permanent fund for internal improvement." The committee was appointed the same day, — Calhoun, Sheffey of Virginia, Creighton of Ohio, Grosvenor of New York, and Ingham of Pennsylvania. December 23 Calhoun reported a bill [1] setting aside the bonus paid by the Bank, $1,500,000, and the future dividends from Bank stock, "as a fund for constructing roads and canals." February 4 he introduced his bill by a speech, showing that a system of internal improvements was necessary, and could, in certain instances, be created by the national government alone.

" Let it not be forgotten," said Calhoun,[2] with the air of sombre forecast which marked his mind and features, " let it be forever kept in mind, that the extent of our republic exposes us to the greatest of all calamities, next

[1] Annals of Congress, 1816–1817, p. 361.
[2] Annals of Congress, 1816–1817, pp. 853, 854.

to the loss of liberty, and even to that in its consequence, — *disunion*. We are great, and rapidly — I was about to say fearfully — growing. This is our pride and danger, our weakness and our strength. Little does he deserve to be intrusted with the liberties of this people, who does not raise his mind to these truths. We are under the most imperious obligation to counteract every tendency to disunion. . . . If . . . we permit a low, sordid, selfish, and sectional spirit to take possession of this House, this happy scene will vanish. We will divide, and in its consequences will follow misery and despotism."

The Constitutional question Calhoun reserved for the future; he thought it scarcely worth discussion, since the good sense of the States might be relied on to prevent practical evils. Nevertheless he discussed it, and drew sufficient authority from the " general welfare " clause, and from the power to " establish " post-roads. Granting that the Constitution was silent, he saw no restraint on Congress : —

" If we are restricted in the use of our money to the enumerated powers, on what principle can the purchase of Louisiana be justified? . . . If it cannot, then are we compelled either to deny that we had the power to purchase, or to strain some of the enumerated powers to prove our right."

The debate was interesting. Timothy Pickering, with the accumulated experience of seventy years, suggested that the right to regulate commerce among the several States, as in the case of light-houses and beacons, covered the proposed appropriation. Clay supported the bill with his usual energy, avowing that among his strongest motives was the wish to add this new distinction to the Fourteenth Congress, so harshly judged by the people. The chief Constitutional argument against the measure was made by Philip P. Barbour of Virginia; but other members opposed it on different grounds, and chiefly because as long as the internal taxes were still exacted, internal improvements should not be undertaken.

If the final vote was a correct test, Constitutional objections had but little weight with Congress. The bill passed the House, February 8, by the small majority of eighty-six to eighty-four. Of the minority no less than thirty-three were New England Federalists, whose opposition was founded on local and sectional reasons. From the slave States about forty-two votes were given against the bill; but a number of these were Federalist, and others were influenced by peculiar reasons. Two thirds of the Virginians voted against the bill; two thirds of the South Carolinians voted in its favor. Probably not more than twenty-five or thirty members, in the total number of one hundred and seventy, regarded the Constitutional difficulty as fatal to the bill.

In the Senate the bill passed by a vote of twenty to fifteen. Of the minority nine represented New England, and six represented Southern States. Every senator from the Middle States, as well as both senators from Virginia, supported the bill. Both senators from Massachusetts, the Republican Varnum and the Federalist Ashmun, opposed it; while Jeremiah Mason of New Hampshire and Rufus King of New York voted in its favor. The confusion of parties was extreme; but the State-rights school of old Republicans seemed to command not more than five or six votes in thirty-five.

The divisions on this bill seemed to leave no question that Congress by an overwhelming majority regarded the Constitutional point as settled. No one doubted that the Judiciary held the same opinion. The friends of the bill had reason to feel secure in regard to the Constitutional issue if on nothing else, and were the more disappointed when, March 3, President Madison exercised for the last time his official authority by returning the bill with a veto founded on Constitutional objections.

"The power to regulate commerce among the several States," he said, "cannot include a power to construct roads and canals, and to improve the navigation of water-courses in order to facilitate, improve, and secure such a commerce, without a latitude of construction departing from the ordinary import of the terms, strengthened by the known inconveniences which doubtless led to the grant of this remedial power to Congress. To refer the power in question to the clause ' to provide for the common defence and general welfare ' would be contrary to the established and consistent rules of interpretation, as rendering the special and careful enumeration of powers which follow the clause nugatory and improper. Such a view of the Constitution would have the effect of giving to Congress a general power of legislation."

Every one who looked at the Constitution as an
instrument or machine to be employed for the first
time, must have admitted that Madison was right.
Interpreted by no other aid than its own terms and
the probable intent of a majority of the Convention which framed and the States which adopted it,
the Constitution contained, and perhaps had been
intended to contain, no power over internal improvements.   The wide difference of opinion which so
suddenly appeared between the President and Congress could not have been the result so much of
different views of the Constitution, as of conclusions
reached since the Constitution was framed.   Congress held the bill to be Constitutional, not because
it agreed with the strict interpretation of the text,
but because it agreed with the interpretation which
for sixteen years the Republican party, through Congress and Executive, had imposed upon the text.

On that point Calhoun's argument left no doubt;
and his question — the last of his speculations preg-
nant with future history — echoed unanswered : " On
what principle can the purchase of Louisiana be
justified ?"   Dismissing all other violations or violence offered to the Constitution by President Madison or his predecessors, — such as the Bank, the
Embargo, the Enforcement laws, the laws for the
government of Orleans Territory, the seizure of West
Florida, — Calhoun's question went to the heart of
the issue between President and Congress.

From the Virginia side only one answer was possible. In returning to their early views of resistance to centralization, Madison and Jefferson must have maintained the invalidity of precedents to affect the Constitution. The veto seemed to create a new classification of public acts into such as were Constitutional; such as were unconstitutional, but still valid; and such as were both unconstitutional and invalid. The admitted validity of an act, like the purchase of Louisiana, even though it were acknowledged to be unconstitutional, did not create a precedent which authorized a repetition of a similar act.

Viewed only from a political standpoint, the veto marked the first decided reaction against the centralizing effect of the war. Unfortunately for the old Republican party, whose principles were thus for a second time to be adopted in appearance by a majority of the people, sixteen years had affected national character; and although precedents might not bind Congress or Executive, they marked the movement of society.

The Veto Message of March 3, 1817, was Madison's Farewell Address. The next day he surrendered to Monroe the powers of government, and soon afterward retired to Virginia, to pass, with his friend Jefferson, the remaining years of a long life, watching the results of his labors.

CHAPTER VII.

THE Union, which contained 5,300,000 inhabitants in 1800, numbered 7,240,000 in 1810, and 9,634,000 in 1820. At the close of Madison's Administration, in 1817, the population probably numbered not less than 8,750,000 persons. The average rate of annual increase was about three and five-tenths per cent, causing the population to double within twenty-three years.

The rate of increase was not uniform throughout the country, but the drift of population was well defined. In 1800 the five New England States contained about 1,240,000 persons. Virginia and North Carolina, united, then contained nearly 1,360,000, or ten per cent more than New England. In 1820 the two groups were still nearer equality. New England numbered about 1,665,000 ; the two Southern States numbered 1,700,000, or about two per cent more than New England. While these two groups, containing nearly half the population of the Union, increased only as one hundred to one hundred and twenty-nine, the middle group, comprising New York, New Jersey, and Pennsylvania, increased in the relation of one hundred to one hundred and ninety-two, — from

1,402,000 in 1800, to 2,696,000 in 1820. Their rate was about the average ratio for the Union; and the three Western States, — Ohio,. Kentucky, and Tennessee, — grew proportionally faster. Their population of 370,000 in 1800 became 1,567,000 in 1820, in the ratio of one hundred to four hundred and twenty-three.

Careful study revealed a situation alarming to New England and Virginia. If only Connecticut, Rhode Island, and Massachusetts, without its district of Maine, were considered, a total population numbering 742,000 in 1800 increased only to 881,000 in 1820, or in the ratio of one hundred to one hundred and eighteen in twenty years. If only the white population of Virginia and North Carolina were taken into the estimate, omitting the negroes, 852,000 persons in 1800 increased to 1,022,000 in 1820, or in the ratio of one hundred to one hundred and twenty. Maryland showed much the same result, while Delaware, which rose from 64,270 in 1800 to 72,674 in 1810, remained stationary, numbering only 72,749 in 1820, — a gain of seventy-five persons in ten years. The white population showed a positive decrease, from 55,361 in 1810 to 55,282 in 1820.

Probably a census taken in 1817 would have given results still less favorable to the sea-coast. The war affected population more seriously than could have been reasonably expected, and stopped the growth of the large cities. New York in 1800 contained 60,000 persons; in 1810 it contained 96,400, but a corpora-

tion census of 1816 reported a population of only
one hundred thousand, although two of the six years
were years of peace and prosperity. From that time
New York grew rapidly, numbering 124,000 in 1820,
— a gain of about twenty-five per cent in four years.
Even the interior town of Albany, which should have
been stimulated by the war, and which increased
four thousand in population between 1800 and 1810,
increased only three thousand between 1810 and
1820. Philadelphia fared worse, for its population of
96,000 in 1810 grew only to 108,000 in 1820, and
fell rapidly behind New York. Baltimore grew from
26,000 in 1800 to 46,000 in 1810, and numbered
less than 63,000 in 1820. Boston suffered more than
Baltimore; for its population, which numbered 24,000
in 1800, grew only to 32,000 in 1810, and numbered
but 43,000 in 1820. Charleston was still more unfortunate. In 1800 its population numbered about
eighteen thousand; in 1810, 24,700; in 1817 a local
census reported a decrease to 23,950 inhabitants, and
the national census of 1820 reported 24,780, or eighty
persons more than in 1810. The town of Charleston
and the State of Delaware increased together by the
same numbers.

Although the war lasted less than three years, its
effect was so great in checking the growth of the
cities that during the period from 1810 to 1820 the
urban population made no relative increase. During
every other decennial period in the national history
the city population grew more rapidly than that of

the rural districts; but between 1810 and 1820 it remained stationary, at four and nine-tenths per cent of the entire population. While Boston, Philadelphia, and Charleston advanced slowly, and New York only doubled its population in twenty years, Western towns like Pittsburg, Cincinnati, and Louisville grew rapidly and steadily, and even New Orleans, though exposed to capture, more than trebled in size; but the Western towns were still too small to rank as important. Even in 1820 the only cities which contained a white population of more than twenty thousand were New York, Philadelphia, Baltimore, and Boston.

The severest sufferers from this situation were the three southern States of New England, — Connecticut, Rhode Island, and Massachusetts, excluding the district of Maine, which was about to become a separate State. Fortunately the northern part of New England, notwithstanding the war, increased much more rapidly than the southern portion; but this increase was chiefly at the cost of Massachusetts, and returned little in comparison with the loss. The situation of Massachusetts and Connecticut was dark. Had not wealth increased more rapidly than population, Massachusetts would have stood on the verge of ruin; yet even from the economical point of view, the outlook was not wholly cheerful.

Judged by the reports of Massachusetts banks, the increase of wealth was surprising. The official returns of 1803, the first year when such returns were made, reported seven banks in the State, with a capi-

tal of $2,225,000 and deposits of $1,500,000. In June,
1816, twenty-five banks returned capital stock amounting nearly to $11,500,000 and deposits of $2,133,000.
The deposits were then small, owing to the decline
of industry and drain of specie that followed the
peace, but the capital invested in banks had more
than quintupled in thirteen years.

This multiplication was not a correct measure of
the general increase in wealth. Indeed, the banks
were in excess of the public wants after the peace,
and their capital quickly shrunk from $11,500,000 in
June, 1816, to $9,300,000 in June, 1817, a decline of
nearly twenty per cent in a year. From that time it
began to increase again, and held its improvement
even in the disastrous year 1819. Assuming 1803
and 1817 as the true terms of the equation, the
banking capital of Massachusetts increased in fourteen years from $2,225,000 to $9,300,000, or more
than quadrupled.

Gauged by bank discounts the increase of wealth
was not so great. In 1803 the debts due to the
banks were returned at $3,850,000 ; in June, 1817,
they were $12,650,000. If the discounts showed the
true growth of industry, the business of the State
somewhat more than trebled in fourteen years.
Probably the chief industries that used the increased
banking capital were the new manufactures, for the
older sources of Massachusetts wealth showed no
equivalent gain. Tested by the imports, the improvement was moderate. In 1800 the gross amount

of duties collected in Massachusetts was less than
$3,200,000; in 1816 it somewhat exceeded $6,100,000,
but had not permanently doubled in sixteen years.
Tested by exports of domestic produce, Massachusetts
showed no gain. In 1803 the value of such produce
amounted to $5,400,000; in 1816, to $5,008,000.[1]

Other methods of calculating the increase of wealth
gave equally contradictory results. The registered
tonnage of Massachusetts engaged in foreign trade
exceeded two hundred and ten thousand tons in
1800; in 1816 it was two hundred and seventy-four
thousand tons. In the coasting-trade Massachusetts
employed seventy-five thousand tons in 1800, and one
hundred and twenty-nine thousand in 1816. The
tonnage employed in the fisheries showed no growth.
The shipping of Massachusetts seemed to indicate an
increase of about forty per cent in sixteen years.

The system of direct taxation furnished another
standard of comparison. In 1798 a valuation was
made in certain States of houses and lands for direct
taxes; another was made in 1813; a third in 1815.
That of 1798 amounted to eighty-four million dollars for Massachusetts; that of 1813, to one hundred
and forty-nine millions; that of 1815, to one hundred and forty-three millions, — a gain of seventy
per cent in sixteen years; but such a valuation in
1817 would probably have shown a considerable loss
on that of 1815.

Evidently the chief increase in wealth consisted in

[1] Pitkin, pp. 55-56.

the growth of manufactures, but after the prostration
of the manufacturing interest in 1816 no plausible
estimate of their true value could be made, unless
the bank discounts measured their progress.   The
result of the whole inquiry, though vague, suggested
that wealth had increased in Massachusetts more
rapidly than population, and had possibly gained
seventy or eighty per cent in sixteen years ; [1] but in
spite of this increase the State was in a pitiable
situation.   Neither steamboats, canals, nor roads
could help it.   Thousands of its citizens migrated to
New York and Ohio, beyond the possibility of future
advantage to the land they left.   Manufactures were
prostrate.   Shipping was driven from the carrying
trade.   Taxation weighed far more heavily than ever
before.   A load of obloquy rested on the State on
account of its war policy and the Hartford Convention.   The national government treated it with severity, and refused to pay for the Massachusetts militia
called into service by the President during the war,
because the governor had refused to place them
under national officers.

The condition of Massachusetts and Maine was a
picture of New England.   Democratic Rhode Island
suffered equally with Federalist Connecticut.   Maine,
New Hampshire, and Vermont showed growth, but
the chief possibility of replacing lost strength lay in
immigration.   During the European wars, no considerable number of immigrants were able to reach

[1] Pitkin, p. 373.

the United States; but immediately after the return
of peace, emigration from Europe to America began
on a scale as alarming to European governments as
the movement to western New York and Ohio was
alarming to the seaboard States of the Union. During the year 1817 twenty-two thousand immigrants
were reported as entering the United States.[1] Twelve
or fourteen thousand were probably Irish; four thousand were German. More than two thousand arrived
in Boston, while about seven thousand landed in New
York and the same number in Philadelphia. The
greater part probably remained near where they
landed, and in some degree supplied the loss of
natives who went west. The rapid growth of the
northern cities of the sea-coast began again only with
the flood of immigration.

Although the three southern States of New England were the severest sufferers, the Virginia group —
comprising Delaware, Maryland, Virginia, and North
Carolina — escaped little better. In twenty years
their white population increased nineteen and five
tenths per cent, while that of Massachusetts, Connecticut, and Rhode Island increased eighteen per
cent. The wealth of Southern States consisted largely
in slaves; and the negro population of the Virginia
group increased about twenty-five per cent in numbers during the sixteen years from 1800 to 1816.
The exports of domestic produce increased about
forty per cent in value, comparing the average of

[1] Niles, 1817.

1801–1805 with that of 1815–1816. The net revenue collected in Virginia increased nearly seventy
per cent, comparing the year 1815 with the average
of the five years 1800–1804 ; while that collected in
North Carolina more than doubled.

Measured by these standards, the growth of wealth
in the Virginia group of States was not less rapid
than in Massachusetts, and the same conclusion was
established by other methods. In 1816 Virginia
contained two State banks, with branches, which
returned for January 1 a capital stock of $4,590,000,
with a note circulation of $6,000,000, and deposits
approaching $2,500,000. Their discounts amounted
to $7,768,000 in January, 1816, and were contracted
to $6,128,000 in the following month of November.[1]
Although Virginia used only half the banking capital
and credits required by Massachusetts, the rate of
increase was equally rapid, and the tendency toward
banking was decided. In 1817 the legislature created
two new banks, one for the valley of Virginia, the
other for western Virginia, with a capital stock of
$600,000, and branches with capital stock of $100,000
for each. Between 1800 and 1817, banking capital
exceeding five million dollars was created in Virginia,
where none had existed before.

If the estimates made by Timothy Pitkin, the best
statistician of the time, were correct, the returns for
direct taxes showed a greater increase of wealth in
Virginia than in Massachusetts.[2] The valuation of

[1] Niles, ix. 427; xi. 196.   [2] Pitkin, p. 372.

Virginia for 1799 was $71,000,000 ; that of 1815 was $165,000,000. The valuation of North Carolina in 1799 was $30,000,000 ; that of 1815 was $51,000,000. Maryland was estimated at $32,000,-000 in 1799, at $106,000,000 in 1815. The average increase for the three States was in the ratio of one hundred to two hundred and forty, while that for Massachusetts, Rhode Island, and Connecticut was nearer one hundred to one hundred and seventy-five. The normal increase for the Union was in the ratio of one hundred to two hundred and sixty-three.

The result obtained from the estimates for direct taxes was affected by a doubt in regard to the correctness of the valuation of 1799, which was believed to have been too low in the Southern States ; but the general conclusion could not be doubted that the Virginia group of States increased steadily in wealth. The rapidity of increase was concealed by an equally rapid impoverishment of the old tobacco-planting aristocracy, whose complaints drowned argument. As the lands of the ancient families became exhausted, the families themselves fell into poverty, or emigrated to the richer Ohio valley. Their decline or departure gave rise to many regrets and alarms. With the impressions thus created, the people associated the want of economical machinery as a cause of their backwardness, and became clamorous for roads, canals, and banks. The revolution in their ideas between 1800 and 1816 was complete.

The North Carolinians were first to denounce their

old habits of indifference, and to declare their State
in danger of ruin on that account. A committee of
the State legislature reported Nov. 30, 1815, that vigorous measures for self-protection could no longer
be postponed : [1] —

"With an extent of territory sufficient to maintain
more than ten millions of inhabitants, . . . we can only
boast of a population something less than six hundred
thousand, and it is but too obvious that this population
under the present state of things already approaches its
maximum. Within twenty-five years past more than two
hundred thousand of our inhabitants have removed to the
waters of the Ohio, Tennessee, and Mobile ; and it is mortifying to witness the fact that thousands of our wealthy
and respectable citizens are annually moving to the West,
. . . and that thousands of our poorer citizens follow them,
being literally driven away by the prospect of poverty.
In this state of things our agriculture is at a stand."

The Virginians showed an equally strong sense of
their perils. Twelve months after the North Carolina legislature took the matter in hand, a committee
of the Virginia legislature in December, 1816, discussed the same topic and reached the same conclusion.[2] Although something had been done by
corporations to open canals on the Potomac, the
James River, and to the Dismal Swamp, the State
of Virginia had in sixteen years made little advance
in material welfare. While New England had built
turnpikes wherever a profit could be expected, in

[1] Niles, ix., Supplement, p. 165.
[2] Niles, ix., Supplement, p. 149.

Virginia, said the committee, "the turnpike-roads of the Commonwealth, except a few short passes of particular mountains and a road recently begun from Fredericksburg to the Blue Ridge, are confined principally to the county of Loudon, the adjacent counties of Fairfax, Fauquier, and Frederick, and to the vicinity of the seat of government." In other respects the situation was worse.

"While many other States," said the committee,[1] "have been advancing in wealth and numbers with a rapidity which has astonished themselves, the ancient Dominion and elder sister of the Union has remained stationary. A very large proportion of her western territory is yet unimproved, while a considerable part of her eastern has receded from its former opulence. How many sad spectacles do her low-lands present of wasted and deserted fields, of dwellings abandoned by their proprietors, of churches in ruins! The genius of her ancient hospitality, benumbed by the cold touch of penury, spreads his scanty hoard in naked halls, or seeks a coarser but more plenteous repast in the lonely cabins of the West. The fathers of the land are gone where another outlet to the ocean turns their thoughts from the place of their nativity, and their affections from the haunts of their youth."

Another committee reported to the House of Delegates Jan. 5, 1816, in favor of extending the banking system of the State.[2] The report used language new as an expression of Virginian opinions.

---

[1] Niles, ix., Supplement, p. 150.
[2] Niles, ix., Supplement, p. 155.

"Your committee believe that a prejudice has gone abroad, which they confidently trust experience will prove to be unfounded even to the satisfaction of those by whom it is entertained, that the policy of Virginia is essentially hostile to commerce and to the rights of commercial men. Upon the removal of this prejudice must depend the future contributions of this Commonwealth toward the prosperity and glory if not the happiness and safety of the United States. Without the confidence of foreigners there can exist no foreign commerce. Without foreign commerce there can exist neither ships, seamen, nor a navy; and a tremendous lesson has taught Virginia that without a navy she can have no security for her repose."

Notwithstanding the gloom of these recitals, the evidence tended to show that while the white population of Virginia increased only about nineteen per cent in sixteen years, its wealth nearly doubled. Comparison with the quicker growth of the Middle States — New York, New Jersey, and Pennsylvania — caused much of the uneasiness felt by New England and Virginia. The banking capital of New York, which probably did not much exceed three million dollars in 1800, amounted in 1816 to nearly $19,000,000; that of Pennsylvania exceeded $16,-000,000. The valuation of houses and lands for the direct tax rose in New York from $100,000,000 in 1799 to nearly $270,000,000 in 1815; and in Pennsylvania, from $102,000,000 in 1799 to $346,000,000 in 1815.[1] The net revenue collected in New York

[1] Pitkin, p. 372.

was $2,700,000 in 1800, and $14,500,000 in 1815; that collected in Pennsylvania was $1,350,000 in 1800, and $7,140,000 in 1815. This rate of increase did not extend to exports. The value of the domestic exports from New York in 1803 was about $7,500,000; in 1816 it exceeded $14,000,000; while the value of Pennsylvanian exports increased little, — being $4,021,000 in 1803 and $4,486,000 in 1816. The population of New York doubled while that of Massachusetts and Virginia hardly increased one third. Pennsylvania grew less rapidly in numbers, but still about twice as fast as New England.

Although this rate of progress seemed to leave New England and Virginia far behind the Middle States, it was less striking than the other economical changes already accomplished or foreseen. The movement of population or of wealth was not so important as the methods by which the movement was effected. The invention of the steamboat gave a decisive advantage to New York over every rival. Already in 1816 the system had united New York city so closely with distant places that a traveller could go from New York to Philadelphia by steamboat and stage in thirteen hours; or to Albany in twenty-four hours; and taking stage to Whitehall in twelve hours could reach Montreal in thirty hours, and go on to Quebec in twenty-four hours, — thus consuming about five and a half successive days in the long journey from Philadelphia to Quebec, sleeping comfortably on his way, and all at an expense of

fifty dollars. This economy of time and money was a
miracle; but New York could already foresee that it
led to other advantages of immeasurable value. The
steamboat gave impetus to travel, and was a blessing
to travellers; but its solid gain for the prosperity of
the United States lay not in passenger traffic so
much as in freight, and New York was the natural
centre of both.

While Pennsylvania, Virginia, and the Carolinas
were building roads and canals across a hundred miles
of mountains, only to reach at last an interior region
which enjoyed an easier outlet for freight, New York
had but to people a level and fertile district, nowhere
fifty miles from navigable water, in order to reach
the great Lake system, which had no natural outlet
within the Union except through the city of New
York. So obvious was the idea of a canal from the
Lakes to the Hudson that it was never out of men's
minds, even before the war; and no sooner did peace
return than the scheme took large proportions. Active leaders of both political parties pressed the plan,
— De Witt Clinton, Gouverneur Morris, and Peter B.
Porter were all concerned in it; but the legislature
and people then supposed that so vast an undertak-
ing as a canal to connect Lake Erie with the ocean,
national in character and military in its probable
utility, required national aid. Supposing the Administration to be pledged to the policy outlined by
Gallatin and approved by Jefferson in the Annual
Message of 1806, the New York commissioners applied

to Congress for assistance, and uniting with other local interests procured the passage of Calhoun's bill for internal improvements.

They were met by Madison's veto. This act, although at first it seemed to affect most the interests of New York, was in reality injurious only to the Southern States. Had the government lent its aid to the Erie Canal, it must have assisted similar schemes elsewhere, and in the end could hardly have refused to carry out Gallatin's plan of constructing canals from the Chesapeake to the Ohio, and from the Santee to the Tennessee River. The veto disappointed New York only for the moment, but was fatal to Southern hopes. After the first shock of discouragement, the New York legislature determined to persevere, and began the work without assistance. The legislature of Pennsylvania at the same time appropriated half a million dollars for roads and canals, and for improvements of river navigation, devoting nearly one hundred and fifty thousand dol lars to aid the turnpike-road to Pittsburg. The fund established by the State of Ohio, as a condition of its admission to the Union, had in 1816 produced means to construct the National or Cumberland Road to the hundred and thirteenth mile. The indifference to internal improvements which had been so marked a popular trait in 1800, gave place to universal interest and activity in 1816; but the Middle States were far in advance of the Eastern and Southern in opening communications with the West; and New York, owing

in no small degree to the veto, could already foresee the time when it would wrest from Pennsylvania
the supply of the valley of the Ohio, while expanding
new tributary territory to an indefinite extent along
the Lakes.

When Madison retired from the Presidency, the
limits of civilization, though rapidly advancing, were
still marked by the Indian boundary, which extended
from the western end of Lake Erie across Indiana,
Kentucky, Tennessee, and the Southwestern territory.
Only weak and helpless tribes remained east of the
Mississippi, waiting until the whites should require
the surrender of their lands; but the whites, already
occupying land far in advance of their needs, could
not yet take the whole. Not until 1826 were the
Indian titles generally extinguished throughout Indiana. The military work was done, and the short
space of sixteen years had practically accomplished
the settlement of the whole country as far as the
Mississippi; but another generation was needed in
order to take what these sixteen years had won.

As population spread, the postal service struggled
after it. Except on the Hudson River, steamboats
were still irregular in their trips; and for this reason
the mails continued to be carried on horseback through
the interior. In 1801 the number of post-offices was
957; in 1817 it was 3,459. In 1801 the length of
post-roads was less than 25,000 miles; in 1817 it was
52,689. In 1800 the gross receipts from postage were
$280,000; in 1817 they slightly exceeded $1,000,000.

In each case the increase much surpassed the ratio for population, and offered another means for forming some estimate of the increase of wealth. The Fourteenth Congress pressed the extension of post-routes in western New York, Ohio, and Indiana; but none was yet established beyond the Mississippi. Rapidity of motion was also increased on the main routes. From New York to Buffalo, four hundred and seventy-five miles, the traveller went at an average rate of five miles an hour, and, sleeping every night, he arrived in about four days. Between Philadelphia and Pittsburg, where no watercourse shortened the distance, the stage-coach consumed five and a half days, allowing for stoppage at night. These rates of travel were equal to those common on routes of similar length in Europe; but long after 1817 the mail from Washington to New Orleans, by a route 1,380 miles in length, required twenty-four days of travel.

Had the steamboat system been at once perfected, the mail could have been carried with much more rapidity; but the progress of the new invention was slow. After the trial trip of the " Clermont," Aug. 17, 1807, five years elapsed before the declaration of war; yet in 1812 New York possessed no other steam-line than the Albany packets. Steam-ferries plied to Hoboken, Amboy, and other places in the immediate neighborhood; but neither Newport, New London, nor New Haven enjoyed steam communication with New York until after the war. In the spring of 1813 eight or nine steamboats belonged to the city of New

York, but only three, which ran to Albany, were
more than ferries. At the same time Philadelphia
possessed six such ferry-boats. From Baltimore a
steamer ran to the head of Chesapeake Bay; but the
southern coast and the town of Charleston saw no
steamboat until a year after the war was ended.

The West was more favored. In 1811 a boat of
four hundred tons was built at Pittsburg and sent
down the river to New Orleans, where it plied between
New Orleans and Natchez. Two more were built at
the same place in 1813–1814; and one of them, the
"Vesuvius," went down the river in the spring of
1814, rousing general interest in the midst of war
by making the trip in nine days and a half, or two
hundred and twenty-seven hours. The "Vesuvius"
remained on the Mississippi for the next two years,
but was burned with her cargo in the summer of
1816. By that time the world was thinking much
of steamboats, and their use was rapidly extending,
though regular trips were still uncommon except in
the east.

The result of the sixteen years, considered only in
the economical development of the Union, was decisive. Although population increased more rapidly
than was usual in human experience, wealth accumulated still faster. From such statistics as the times
afforded, a strong probability has been shown that
while population doubled within twenty-three years,
wealth doubled within twenty. Statistics covering
the later period of national growth, warrant the

belief that a valuation of $1,742,000,000 in 1800 corresponded to a valuation of $3,734,000,000 in 1820; and that if a valuation of $328 per capita is assumed for 1800, a valuation of $386 per capita may be estimated for 1820.[1]

These sixteen years set at rest the natural doubts that had attended the nation's birth. The rate of increase both in population and wealth was established and permanent, unless indeed it should become even more rapid. Every serious difficulty which seemed alarming to the people of the Union in 1800 had been removed or had sunk from notice in 1816. With the disappearance of every immediate peril, foreign or domestic, society could devote all its energies, intellectual and physical, to its favorite objects. This result was not the only or even the chief proof that economical progress was to be at least as rapid in the future as at the time when the nation had to struggle with political difficulties. Not only had the people during these sixteen years escaped from dangers, they had also found the means of supplying their chief needs. Besides clearing away every obstacle to the occupation and development of their continent as far as the Mississippi River, they created the steamboat, the most efficient instrument yet conceived for developing such a country. The continent lay before them, like an uncovered ore-bed. They could see, and they could even calculate with reasonable accu-

[1] The Wealth of the United States and the Rate of its Increase. By Henry Gannett, International Review, May, 1882.

racy, the wealth it could be made to yield. With almost the certainty of a mathematical formula, knowing the rate of increase of population and of wealth, they could read in advance their economical history for at least a hundred years.

CHAPTER VIII.

THE movement of thought, more interesting than the movement of population or of wealth, was equally well defined. In the midst of political dissension and economical struggles, religion still took precedence; and the religious movement claimed notice not merely for its depth or for its universality, but also and especially for its direction. Religious interest and even excitement were seen almost everywhere, both in the older and in the newer parts of the country; and every such movement offered some means of studying or illustrating the development of national character. For the most part the tendency seemed emotional rather than intellectual; but in New England the old intellectual pre-eminence, which once marked the Congregational clergy, developed a quality both new and distinctive.

The Congregational clergy, battling with the innate vices of human nature, thought themselves obliged to press on their hearers the consequences of God's infinite wrath rather than those of his infinite love. They admitted that in a worldly sense they erred, and they did not deny that their preaching sometimes leaned to severity; but they would have been

false to their charge and undeserving of their high
character had they lost sight of their radical doctrine
that every man was by nature personally depraved,
and unless born again could not hope to see the
kingdom of God.   Many intellectual efforts had been
made by many ages of men to escape the logic of
this doctrine, but without success.   The dogma and
its consequences could not be abandoned without
abandoning the Church.

From this painful dilemma a group of young Boston clergymen made a new attempt to find a path of
escape.   Their movement drew its inspiration from
Harvard College, and was simultaneous with the sway
of Jefferson's political ideas; but the relationship
which existed between religious and political innovation was remote and wholly intellectual.   Harvard
College seemed to entertain no feeling toward Jefferson but antipathy, when in 1805 the corporation appointed Henry Ware, whose Unitarian tendencies were
well known, to be Hollis Professor of Theology.   The
Unitarianism of Henry Ware and his supporters implied at that time no well-defined idea beyond a qualified rejection of the Trinity, and a suggestion of what
they thought a more comprehensible view of Christ's
divine character; but it still subverted an essential
dogma of the Church, and opened the way to heresy.
The Calvinists could no longer regard Harvard College as a school proper for the training of clergy; and
they were obliged to establish a new theological semi-
nary, which they attached to a previously existing

Academy at Andover, in Essex County, Massachusetts. The two branches of the New England Calvinists — known then as old Calvinism and Hopkinsianism — united in framing for the instructors of the Andover school a creed on the general foundation of the Westminster Assembly's Shorter Catechism, and thus provided for the future education of their clergy in express opposition to Unitarians and Universalists.

Thenceforward the theological school of Harvard College became more and more Unitarian. The Massachusetts parishes, divided between the two schools of theology, selected, as pleased a majority of their church-members, either Orthodox or Unitarian pastors ; and while the larger number remained Calvinistic, though commonly preferring ministers who avoided controversy, the Boston parishes followed the Unitarian movement, and gradually filled their pulpits with young men. The Unitarian clergy soon won for themselves and for their city a name beyond proportion with their numbers.

Joseph Stevens Buckminster, the first, and while he lived the most influential, of these preachers, began his career in 1805 by accepting a call from one of the old Boston churches. He died in 1812 at the close of his twenty-eighth year. His influence was rather social and literary than theological or controversial. During his lifetime the Unitarian movement took no definite shape, except as a centre of revived interest in all that was then supposed to be best and purest in religious, literary, and artistic feeling. After

his death, Unitarians learned to regard William
Ellery Channing as their most promising leader.
Channing had accepted the charge of a Boston church
as early as 1803, and was about four years older than
Buckminster. A third active member of the Boston
clergy was Samuel Cooper Thacher, who took charge
of a Boston parish in 1811, and was five years younger
than Channing. In all, some seven or eight churches
were then called Unitarian; but they professed no
uniform creed, and probably no two clergymen or
parishes agreed in their understanding of the precise
difference between them and the Orthodox church.
Shades of difference distinguished each Unitarian
parish from every other, and the degree of their divergence from the old creed was a subject of constant
interest and private discussion, although the whole
body of churches, Congregational as well as Unitarian,
remained in external repose.

The calm was not broken until the close of the war
relieved New England from a political anxiety which
for fifteen years had restrained internal dissensions.
No sooner did peace restore to New England the
natural course of its intellectual movement than
the inevitable schism broke out. In June, 1815,
the "Panoplist," the mouthpiece of the Congregational clergy, published an article charging the Unitarians with pursuing an unavowed propaganda, and
calling upon the Church to refuse them communion.
Channing and his friends thought the attack to require reply, and, after consultation, Channing pub-

lished a "Letter to the Rev. Samuel C. Thacher,"
which began a discussion and a theological movement
of no slight interest to American history.

Channing's theology at that time claimed no merit
for originality. His letter to Thacher betrayed more
temper than he would afterward have shown; but in
no particular was he more earnest than in repelling
the idea that he or his brethren were innovators. In
whatever points they disagreed, they were most nearly
unanimous in repudiating connection with the English Unitarians who denied the divinity of Christ.
Channing declared " that a majority of our brethren
believe that Jesus Christ is more than man; that he
existed before the world ; that he literally came from
heaven to save our race; that he sustains other offices
than those of a teacher and witness to the truth ; and
that he still acts for our benefit, and is our intercessor
with the Father." So far was Channing from wishing to preach a new theology that he would gladly
have accepted the old had he thought it intelligible :

"It is from deep conviction that I have stated once and
again that the differences between Unitarians and Trinitarians lie more in sounds than in ideas ; that a barbarous
phraseology is the chief wall of partition between these
classes of Christians; and that could Trinitarians tell
us what they mean, their system would generally be
found little else than a mystical form of the Unitarian
doctrine."

Calvinists could not be blamed for thinking that
their venerable creed, the painful outcome of the

closest and most strenuous reasoning known in the
Christian world, was entitled to more respect than to
be called "little else than a mystical form of the
Unitarian doctrine." The Unitarians themselves
scarcely attempted to make the infinite more intelligible to the finite by any new phraseology. They
avowed a dislike for dogma as their merit. During
these early years they systematically avoided controversy ; in the pulpit they never assailed and seldom
mentioned other forms of Christian faith, or even
the scheme of Trinity which caused their schism.

"So deeply are we convinced," said Channing's letter,
"that the great end of preaching is to promote a spirit
of love, a sober, righteous, and godly life, and that every
doctrine is to be urged simply and exclusively for this
end, that we have sacrificed our ease, and have chosen to
be less striking preachers rather than to enter the lists of
controversy."

Yet the popular dislike of Calvinistic severity could
not wholly make good the want of doctrinal theology.
The Unitarian clergy, however unwilling to widen
the breach between themselves and the old Church,
were ill at ease under the challenges of Orthodox
critics, and could not escape the necessity of defining
their belief.

"According to your own concession," rejoined Dr.
Samuel Worcester to Channing's letter, "the party in
whose behalf you plead generally deny the essential
divinity of the Saviour, and hold him to be a being entirely 'distinct from God,' entirely 'dependent,' — in

other words, a mere creature. . . . You doubtless do not suppose that by any mere creature atonement could be made for the sins of an apostate world of sufficient merit for the pardon, sanctification, and eternal salvation of all who should trust in him ; therefore if you hold to atonement in any sense, yet unquestionably not in the sense of a proper propitiatory sacrifice. Upon this denial of atonement must follow of course the denial of pardon procured by the blood of Christ, of justification through faith in him, of redemption from eternal death unto everlasting life by him. Connected, and generally if not invariably concomitant, with the denial of these doctrines is a denial of the Holy Spirit in his personal character and offices, and of the renewal of mankind unto holiness by his sovereign agency, as held by Orthodox Christians. Now, sir, are these small and trivial points of difference between you and us? "

Channing protested against these inferences ; but he did not deny — indeed, he affirmed — that Unitarians regarded dogma as unnecessary to salvation. "In our judgment of professed Christians," he replied, " we are guided more by their temper and lives than by any peculiarities of opinion. We lay it down as a great and indisputable opinion, clear as the sun at noonday, that the great end for which Christian truth is revealed is the sanctification of the soul, the formation of the Christian character ; and wherever we see the marks of this character displayed in a professed disciple of Jesus, we hope, and rejoice to hope, that he has received all the truth which is necessary to his salvation." The hope might help to soothe anxiety and distress, but it defied conclusions reached by the most anxious and often renewed labors of churchmen for eighteen hundred years. Something more than a hope was necessary as the foundation of a faith.

Not until the year 1819, did Channing quit the cautious attitude he at first assumed. Then, in his " Sermon on the Ordination of Jared Sparks " at Baltimore, he accepted the obligation to define his relation to Christian doctrine, and with the support of Andrews Norton, Henry Ware, and other Unitarian clergymen gave a doctrinal character to the movement. With this phase of his influence the present story has nothing to do. In the intellectual development of the country, the earlier stage of Unitarianism was more interesting than the later, for it marked a general tendency of national thought. At a time when Boston grew little in population and but moderately in wealth, and when it was regarded with antipathy, both political and religious, by a vast majority of the American people, its society had never been so agreeable or so fecund. No such display of fresh and winning genius had yet been seen in America as was offered by the genial outburst of intellectual activity in the early days of the Unitarian schism. No more was heard of the Westminster doctrine that man had lost all ability of will to any spiritual good accompanying salvation, but was dead in sin. So strong was the reaction against old dogmas that for thirty years society seemed less likely to resume the ancient faith in the Christian Trinity

than to establish a new Trinity, in which a deified
humanity should have place. Under the influence of
Channing and his friends, human nature was adorned
with virtues hardly suspected before, and with hopes
of perfection on earth altogether strange to theology.
The Church then charmed. The worth of man became under Channing's teachings a source of pride
and joy, with such insistence as to cause his hearers
at last to recall, almost with a sense of relief, that
the Saviour himself had been content to regard them
only as of more value than many sparrows.

The most remarkable quality of Unitarianism was
its high social and intellectual character. The other
more popular religious movements followed for the
most part a less ambitious path, but were marked
by the same humanitarian tendency. In contrast
with old stringency of thought, the religious activity of the epoch showed warmth of emotion. The
elder Buckminster, a consistent Calvinist clergyman,
settled at Portsmouth in New Hampshire, while
greatly distressed by his son's leanings toward loose
theology, was at the same time obliged to witness
the success of other opinions, which he thought
monstrous, preached by Hosea Ballou, an active
minister in the same town. This new doctrine,
which took the name of Universalism, held as an
article of faith " that there is one God, whose nature
is love, revealed in one Lord Jesus Christ, by one
Holy Spirit of grace, who will finally restore the
whole family of mankind to holiness and happiness."

In former times any one who had publicly professed
belief in universal salvation would not have been
regarded as a Christian. With equal propriety he
might have preached the divinity of Ammon or
Diana. To the old theology one god was as strange
as the other; and so deeply impressed was Dr. Buckminster with this conviction, that he felt himself
constrained in the year 1809 to warn Hosea Ballou
of his error, in a letter pathetic for its conscientious
self-restraint. Yet the Universalists steadily grew
in numbers and respectability, spreading from State
to State under Ballou's guidance, until they became
as well-established and as respectable a church as
that to which Buckminster belonged.

A phenomenon still more curious was seen in the
same year, 1809, in western Pennsylvania. Near
the banks of the Monongahela, in Washington
County, a divergent branch of Scotch Presbyterian-
ism established a small church, and under the
guidance of Thomas Campbell, a recent emigrant
from Scotland, issued, Sept. 7, 1809, a Declaration:

" Being well aware from sad experience of the heinous
nature and pernicious tendency of religious controversy
among Christians, tired and sick of the bitter jarrings
and janglings of a party spirit, we would desire to be at
rest; and were it possible, would also desire to adopt
and recommend such measures as would give rest to our
brethren throughout all the churches, as would restore
unity, peace, and purity to the whole Church of God.
This desirable rest, however, we utterly despair either to
find for ourselves, or to be able to recommend to our

brethren, by continuing amid the diversity and rancor of
party contentions the varying uncertainty and clashings
of human opinions; nor indeed can we reasonably expect
to find it anywhere but in Christ and his simple word,
which is the same yesterday, to-day, and forever.   Our
desire, therefore, for ourselves and our brethren would
be that rejecting human opinions and the inventions of
men as of any authority, or as having any place in the
Church of God, we might forever cease from further
contentions about such things, returning to and holding
fast by the original standard."

Campbell's Declaration expressed so wide a popular
want that his church, in a few years, became one of
the largest branches of the great Baptist persuasion.
Perhaps in these instances of rapid popular grouping,
love of peace was to some extent supplemented by
jealousy of learning, and showed as much spirit of
social independence as of religious instinct.   The
growth of vast popular sects in a democratic community might testify to intellectual stagnation as
well as to religious or social earnestness; but whatever was the amount of thought involved in such
movements, one character was common to them all,
as well as to the Unitarians, — they agreed in relax-
ing the strictness of theological reasoning.   Channing united with Campbell in suggesting that the
Church should ignore what it could not compre-
hend.   In a popular and voluntary form they proposed self-restraints which should have the same
effect as the formal restraints of the hierarchies.
" Rejecting," like Campbell, " human opinions and

the inventions of men," — preaching, like Channing and Ballou, " that there is one God, whose nature is love," and that doctrine was useless except to promote a spirit of love, — they founded new churches on what seemed to resemble an argument that the intellectual difficulties in their path must be unessential because they were insuperable.

Wide as the impulse was to escape the rigor of bonds and relax the severity of thought, organizations so deeply founded as the old churches were not capable of destruction. They had seen many similar human efforts, and felt certain that sooner or later such experiments must end in a return to the old standards. Even the Congregational Church of New England, though reduced in Boston to a shadow of its old authority, maintained itself at large against its swarm of enemies, — Unitarian, Universalist, Baptist, Methodist, — resisting, with force of character and reasoning, the looseness of doctrine and vagueness of thought which marked the time. Yale College remained true to it. Most of the parishes maintained their old relations. If the congregations in some instances crumbled away or failed to increase, the Church could still stand erect, and might reflect with astonishment on its own strength, which survived so long a series of shocks apparently fatal. For half a century the Congregational clergy had struggled to prevent innovation, while the people emigrated by hundreds of thousands in order to innovate. Obliged to insist on the infinite justice rather than on the infinite mercy of God, they shocked the instincts of the new generation, which wanted to enjoy worldly blessings without fear of future reckoning. Driven to bay by the deistic and utilitarian principles of Jefferson's democracy, they fell into the worldly error of defying the national instinct, pressing their resistance to the war until it amounted to treasonable conspiracy. The sudden peace swept away much that was respectable in the old society of America, but perhaps its noblest victim was the unity of the New England Church.

The Church, whether Catholic or Protestant, Lutheran or Calvinistic, always rested in the conviction that every divergence from the great highways of religious thought must be temporary, and that no permanent church was possible except on foundations already established; but the State stood in a position less self-confident. The old principles of government were less carefully developed, and Democrats in politics were more certain than Unitarians or Universalists in theology that their intellectual conclusions made a stride in the progress of thought. Yet the sixteen years with which the century opened were singularly barren of new political ideas. Apparently the extreme activity which marked the political speculations of the period between 1775 and 1800, both in America and in Europe, had exhausted the energy of society, for Americans showed interest only in the practical working of their experiments, and added nothing to the ideas that underlay them. With

such political thought as society produced, these
pages have been chiefly filled ; the result has been
told. The same tendency which in religion led to
reaction against dogma, was shown in politics by
general acquiescence in practices which left un-
settled the disputed principles of government. No
one could say with confidence what theory of the
Constitution had prevailed. Neither party was satisfied, although both acquiesced. While the Legislative and Executive branches of the government
acted on no fixed principle, but established precedents at variance with any consistent theory, the
Judiciary rendered so few decisions that Constitutional law stood nearly still. Only at a later time
did Chief-Justice Marshall begin his great series of
judicial opinions, — McCulloch against the State of
Maryland in 1819 ; Dartmouth College in the same
year ; Cohens against the State of Virginia in 1821.
No sooner were these decisive rulings announced,
than they roused the last combative energies of
Jefferson against his old enemy the Judiciary :
" That body, like gravity, ever acting, with noiseless
foot and unalarming advance, gaining ground step
by step, and holding what it gains, is engulfing
insidiously the special governments."

Marshall had few occasions to decide Constitutional
points during the Administrations of Jefferson and
Madison, but the opinions he gave were emphatic.
When Pennsylvania in 1809 resisted, in the case of
Gideon Olmstead, a process of the Supreme Court,

the chief-justice, without unnecessary words, declared that " if the legislatures of the several States
may at will annul the judgments of the courts of the
United States, and destroy the rights acquired under
those judgments, the Constitution itself becomes
a solemn mockery, and the nation is deprived of the
means of enforcing its laws by the instrumentality of
its own tribunals." Pennsylvania yielded; and Marshall, in the following year, carried a step further the
authority of his court. He overthrew the favorite
dogma of John Randolph and the party of State
rights, so long and vehemently maintained in the
Yazoo dispute.

The Yazoo claims came before the court in the
case of Fletcher against Peck, argued first in 1809
by Luther Martin, J. Q. Adams, and Robert G. Harper; and again in 1810 by Martin, Harper, and
Joseph Story. March 16, 1810, the chief-justice
delivered the opinion. Declining, as " indecent in
the extreme," to enter into an inquiry as to the corruption of " the sovereign power of a State," he dealt
with the issue whether a legislature could annul
rights vested in an individual by a law in its nature
a contract.

" It may well be doubted," he argued, " whether the
nature of society and government does not prescribe
some limits to the legislative power; and if any are to
be prescribed, where are they to be found if the property
of an individual, fairly and honestly acquired, may be
seized without compensation? To the legislature all

legislative power is granted; but the question whether the act of transferring the property of an individual to the public be in the nature of the legislative power, is well worthy of serious reflection. It is the peculiar province of the legislature to prescribe general rules for the government of society : the application of those rules to individuals in society would seem to be the duty of other departments. How far the power of giving the law may involve every other power, in cases where the Constitution is silent, never has been and perhaps never can be definitely stated."

In the case under consideration, Marshall held that the Constitution was not silent. The provision that no State could pass any law impairing the obligation of contracts, as well as " the general principles which are common to our free institutions," restrained the State of Georgia from passing a law whereby the previous contract could be rendered void. His decision settled, as far as concerned the Judiciary, a point regarded as vital by the State-rights school. Four years afterward Congress gave the required compensation for the contract broken by Georgia.

The chief-justice rendered no more leading Constitutional decisions during Madison's term of office ; but his influence was seen in a celebrated opinion delivered by Justice Story in 1816, in the case of Martin against Hunter's Lessee. There the court came in conflict with the State of Virginia. The Court of Appeals of that State refused to obey a mandate of the Supreme Court, alleging that the proceedings of the Supreme Court were *coram non judice,* or beyond its jurisdiction, being founded on section 25 of the Judiciary Act of 1789, which was unconstitutional in extending the appellate jurisdiction of the Supreme Court over the State courts.

The Court of Appeals was unfortunate in the moment of its resistance to the authority of the national courts. While the case was passing through its last stage peace was declared, and the national authority sprang into vigor unknown before. The chief-justice would not with his own hand humiliate the pride of the Court of Appeals, for which as a Virginian and a lawyer he could feel only deep respect. He devolved the unpleasant duty on young Justice Story, whose own State of Massachusetts was then far from being an object of jealousy to Virginia, and who, a Republican in politics, could not be prejudiced by party feeling against the Virginia doctrine. Much of the opinion bore the stamp of Marshall's mind; much showed the turn of Story's intelligence; yet the same principle lay beneath the whole, and no one could detect a divergence between the Federalism of the Virginia chief-justice and the Democracy of the Massachusetts lawyer.

"It has been argued," said the court, "that such an appellate jurisdiction over State courts is inconsistent with the genius of our governments and the spirit of the Constitution; that the latter was never designed to act upon State sovereignties, but only upon the people; and that if the power exists, it will materially impair the sovereignty of the States and the independence of their courts. We cannot yield to the force of this reasoning; it assumes principles which we cannot admit, and draws conclusions to which we do not yield our assent. It is a mistake that the Constitution was not designed to operate upon States in their corporate capacity. It is crowded with provisions which restrain or annul the sovereignty of the States in some of the highest branches of their prerogatives. . . . When, therefore, the States are stripped of some of the highest attributes of sovereignty, and the same are given to the United States; when the legislatures of the States are in some respects under the control of Congress, and in every case are, under the Constitution, bound by the paramount authority of the United States, — it is certainly difficult to support the argument that the appellate power over the decisions of State courts is contrary to the genius of our institutions."

So far were the political principles of the people from having united in a common understanding, that while the Supreme Court of the United States thus differed from the Virginia Court of Appeals in regard to the genius of the government and the spirit of the Constitution, Jefferson still publicly maintained that the national and state governments were " as independent, in fact, as different nations," and that the function of one was foreign, while that of the other was domestic. Madison still declared that Congress could not build a road or clear a watercourse; while Congress believed itself authorized to do both, and in that belief passed a law which Madison vetoed. In politics as in theology, the practical system which

resulted from sixteen years of experience seemed
to rest on the agreement not to press principles to
a conclusion.

No new idea was brought forward, and the old ideas,
though apparently incapable of existing together,
continued to exist in rivalry like that of the dogmas
which perplexed the theological world ; but between
the political and religious movement a distinct difference could be seen.   The Church showed no tendency to unite in any creed or dogma, — indeed, religious society rather tended to more divisions ; but
in politics public opinion slowly moved in a fixed
direction.   The movement could not easily be measured, and was subject to reaction ; but its reality was
shown by the protests of Jefferson, the veto of Madison, and the decisions of the Supreme Court.   No
one doubted that a change had occurred since 1798.
The favorite State-rights dogma of that time had
suffered irreparable injury.   For sixteen years the
national government in all its branches had acted,
without listening to remonstrance, on the rule that
it was the rightful interpreter of its own powers.   In
this assumption the Executive, the Legislature, and
the Judiciary had agreed.   Massachusetts and Pennsylvania, as well as Virginia and Georgia, yielded.
Louisiana had been bought and admitted into the
Union ; the Embargo had been enforced ; one National Bank had been destroyed and another established ; every essential function of a sovereignty had
been performed, without an instance of failure, though

not without question.   However unwilling the minority might be to admit in theory the overthrow of
their principles, every citizen assented in daily practice to the rule that the national government alone
interpreted its own powers in the last resort.   From
the moment the whole people learned to accept the
practice, the dispute over theory lost importance, and
the Virginia Resolutions of 1798 marked only a stage
in the development of a sovereignty.

The nature of the sovereignty that was to be the
result of American political experiment, the amount
of originality which could be infused into an idea so
old, was a matter for future history to settle.   Many
years were likely to elapse before the admitted practice
of the government and people could be fully adopted
into the substance of their law, but the process thus
far had been rapid.   In the brief space of thirty years,
between 1787 and 1817, — a short generation, — the
Union had passed through astonishing stages.   Probably no great people ever grew more rapidly and became more mature in so short a time.   The ideas of
1787 were antiquated in 1815, and lingered only in
districts remote from active movement.   The subsi-
dence of interest in political theories was a measure
of the change, marking the general drift of society
toward practical devices for popular use, within popular intelligence.   The only work that could be said
to represent a school of thought in politics was written
by John Taylor of Caroline, and was probably never
read, — or if read, certainly never understood, — north

of Baltimore by any but curious and somewhat deep students, although to them it had value.

John Taylor of Caroline might without irreverence be described as a *vox clamantis*, — the voice of one crying in the wilderness. Regarded as a political thinker of the first rank by Jefferson, Monroe, John Randolph, and the Virginia school, he admitted, with the geniality of the class to which he belonged, that his disciples invariably deserted in practice the rules they praised in his teaching ; but he continued to teach, and the further his scholars drifted from him the more publicly and profusely he wrote. His first large volume, " An Inquiry into the Principles and Policy of the Government of the United States," published in 1814, during the war, was in form an answer to John Adams's "Defence of the Constitutions" published in London twenty-five years before. In 1787 John Adams, like Jefferson, Hamilton, Madison, Jay, and other constitution-makers, might, without losing the interest of readers, indulge in speculations more or less visionary in regard to the future character of a nation yet in its cradle ; but in 1814 the character of people and government was formed ; the lines of their activity were fixed. A people which had in 1787 been indifferent or hostile to roads, banks, funded debt, and nationality, had become in 1815 habituated to ideas and machinery of the sort on a great scale. Monarchy or aristocracy no longer entered into the public mind as factors in future development. Yet Taylor resumed the discussions of 1787 as though

the interval were a blank; and his only conclusion
from the experience of thirty years was that both
political parties were equally moving in a wrong
direction.

" The two parties, called Republican and Federal," he
concluded, " have hitherto undergone but one revolution.
Yet each when in power preached Filmer's old doctrine
of passive obedience in a new form, with considerable
success; and each, out of power, strenuously contro-
verted it. The party in power asserted that however
absurd or slavish this doctrine was under other forms
of the numerical analysis, the people under ours were
identified (the new term to cog this old doctrine upon the
United States) with the government; and that therefore
an opposition to the government was an opposition to
the nation itself. . . . This identifying doctrine . . .
puts an end to the idea of a responsibility of the government to the nation; . . . it renders useless the freedom
of speech and of the press; it converts the representative
into the principal; it destroys the division of power between the people and the government, as being themselves
indivisible; and in short it is inconsistent with every
principle by which politicians and philosophers have
hitherto defined a free government."

The principle to which Taylor so strenuously objected was nevertheless the chief political result of
national experience. Somewhere or another a point
was always reached where opposition became treasonable,—as Virginia, like Massachusetts, had learned
both when in power and when out. Taylor's speculations ended only in an admission of their own prac-

tical sterility, and his suggestions for restraining the growth of authority assumed the possibility of returning to the conditions of 1787. Banks were his horror. Stocks and bonds, or paper evidences of indebtedness in any form, he thought destructive to sound principles of government. The Virginia and Kentucky Resolutions of 1798 were his best resource for the preservation of civil liberty. However well-founded his fears might be, his correctives could no longer be applied. Political philosophers of all ages were fond of devising systems for imaginary Republics, Utopias, and Oceanas, where practical difficulties could not stand in their way. Taylor was a political philosopher of the same school, and his Oceana on the banks of the Rappahannock was a reflection of his own virtues.

CHAPTER IX.

SOCIETY showed great interest in the statesmen or preachers who won its favor, and earnestly discussed the value of political or religious dogmas, without betraying a wish to subject itself ever again to the rigor of a strict creed in politics or religion. In a similar spirit it touched here and there, with a light hand, the wide circuit of what was called *belles lettres,* without showing severity either in taste or temper.

For the first four or five years of the century, Dennie's " Portfolio" contained almost everything that was produced in the United States under the form of light literature. The volumes of the " Portfolio " for that period had the merit of representing the literary efforts of the time, for Philadelphia insisted on no standard of taste so exacting as to exclude merit, or even dulness, in any literary form. Jacobins, as Dennie called Democrats, were not admitted into the circle of the " Portfolio ; " but Jacobins rarely troubled themselves with *belles lettres.*

The " Portfolio " reflected a small literary class scattered throughout the country, remarkable chiefly for close adhesion to established English ideas. The English standard was then extravagantly Tory, and

the American standard was the same. At first sight
the impression was strange. A few years later, no
ordinary reader could remember that ideas so illib-
eral had seriously prevailed among educated Americans. By an effort, elderly men could, in the next
generation, recall a time when they had been taught
that Oliver Cromwell was a monster of wickedness
and hypocrisy ; but they could hardly believe that at
any period an American critic coldly qualified " Para-
dise Lost," and " Avenge, O Lord, thy slaughtered
saints," as good poetry, though written by a Republican and an enemy of established order. This was
the tone of Dennie's criticism, and so little was it
confined to him that even young Buckminster, in
his Phi Beta Kappa Oration of 1809, which was
regarded as making almost an epoch in American
literature, spoke of Milton's eyes as " quenched in
the service of a vulgar and usurping faction," and of
Milton's life as " a memorable instance of the temporary degradation of learning." Buckminster was
then remonstrating against the influence of politics
upon letters rather than expressing a political sentiment, but his illustration was colored by the general
prejudices of British Toryism. Half a century before,
Dr. Johnson had taken the tone of Tory patronage
toward Milton's genius, and Johnson and Burke were
still received in America as final authorities for correct opinion in morals, literature, and politics. The
" Portfolio " regarded Johnson not only as a " super-
lative " moralist and politician, but also as a " sub-

lime " critic and a " transcendent " poet. Burke and
Cicero stood on the same level, as masters before
whose authority criticism must silently bow.

Yet side by side with these conventional standards,
the " Portfolio " showed tendencies which seemed
inconsistent with conservatism, — a readiness to welcome literary innovations contradicting every established canon. No one would have supposed that
the critic who accepted Johnson and Pope as transcendent poets, should also delight in Burns and
Wordsworth; yet Dennie was unstinted in praise of
poetry which, as literature, was hardly less revolutionary than the writings of Godwin in politics.
Dennie lost no opportunity of praising Coleridge, and
reprinted with enthusiasm the simplest ballads of
Wordsworth. Moore was his personal friend, and
Moore's verses his models. Wherever his political
prejudices were untouched, he loved novelty. He
seemed to respect classical authority only because
it was established, but his literary instincts were
broader than those of Jefferson.

The original matter of the " Portfolio " was naturally unequal, and for the most part hardly better
than that of a college magazine. Dennie was apt to
be commonplace, trivial, and dull. His humor was
heavy and commonly coarse; he allowed himself
entire freedom, and no little grossness of taste. Of
scholarship, or scholarly criticism, his paper showed
great want. He tried to instruct as well as to
amuse, but society soon passed the stage to which his

writing belonged. The circulation of the " Portfolio "
probably never exceeded fifteen hundred copies, and
Dennie constantly complained that the paper barely
supported itself. When the Bostonians, in the year
1805, began to feel the spirit of literary ambition,
they took at once a stride beyond Dennie's power, and
established a monthly magazine called the " Anthology and Boston Review," which in 1806 numbered
four hundred and forty subscribers. The undertak-
ing was doubly remarkable; for the Anthology Society
which supported the Review combined with it the
collection of a library, limited at first to periodical
publications, which expanded slowly into the large
and useful library known as the Boston Athenæum.
The Review and Library quickly became the centre
of literary taste in Boston, and, in the words of
Josiah Quincy many years afterward, might be considered as a revival of polite learning in America.
The claim was not unreasonable, for the Review far
surpassed any literary standards then existing in
the United States, and was not inferior to any in
England ; for neither the Edinburgh nor the Quar-
terly Review was established until several years
later.

The Anthology Society, which accomplished the
feat of giving to Boston for the first time the lead of
American literary effort, consisted largely of clergymen, and represented, perhaps unintentionally, the
coming Unitarian movement. Its president and
controlling spirit had no sympathy with either divi-

sion of the Congregational Church, but was a clergyman of the Church of England.   John Sylvester John Gardiner, the rector of Trinity, occupied a peculiar position in Boston.   Of American descent, but English birth and education, he was not prevented by the isolation of his clerical character from taking an active part in affairs, and his activity was sometimes greater than his discretion.   His political sermons rivalled those of the Congregational ministers Osgood and Parish, in their violence against Jefferson and the national government; his Federalism was that of the Essex Junto, with a more decided leaning to disunion; but he was also an active and useful citizen, ready to take his share in every good work. When he became president of the Anthology Society, he was associated with a clergyman of Unitarian opinions as vice-president, — the Rev. William Emerson, a man of high reputation in his day, but better known in after years as the father of Ralph Waldo Emerson.   The first editor was Samuel Cooper Thacher, to whom, ten years afterward, Channing addressed his earliest controversial letter.   Young Buckminster and William Tudor, a Boston man, who for the next twenty years was active in the literary life of Massachusetts, were also original members. The staff of the "Anthology" was greatly superior to ordinary editorial resources; and in a short time the Review acquired a reputation for ability and sharpness of temper never wholly forgiven.   Its unpopularity was the greater because its aggressiveness

took the form of assaults on Calvinism, which earned
the ill-will of the Congregational clergy.

Buckminster and Channing were the editor's closest friends, and their liberality of thought was remarkable for the time and place; yet the point from
which the liberality of Boston started would have
been regarded in most parts of the Union as conservative. Channing's fear of France and attachment
to England were superstitious.

"I will not say," began his Fast Day Sermon in 1810,
"that the present age is as strongly marked or distinguished from all other ages as that in which Jesus Christ
appeared; but with that single exception, perhaps the
present age is the most eventful the world has ever
known. We live in times which have no parallel in past
ages; in times when the human character has almost
assumed a new form; in times of peculiar calamity, of
thick darkness, and almost of despair. . . . The danger
is so vast, so awful, and so obvious, that the blindness,
the indifference, which prevail argue infatuation, and
give room for apprehension that nothing can rouse us to
those efforts by which alone the danger can be averted.
Am I asked what there is so peculiar and so tremendous
in the times in which we live? . . . I answer: In the
very heart of Europe, in the centre of the civilized world,
a new power has suddenly arisen on the ruins of old
institutions, peculiar in its character, and most ruinous
in its influence."

While Channing felt for France the full horror of
his Federalist principles, he regarded England with
equivalent affection.

" I feel a peculiar interest in England," he explained
in a note appended to the Fast Day Sermon ; " for I
believe that there Christianity is exerting its best influences on the human character ; that there the perfections
of human nature, wisdom, virtue, and piety are fostered
by excellent institutions, and are producing the delight-
ful fruits of domestic happiness, social order, and general
prosperity."

The majority of Americans took a different view
of the subject; but even those who most strongly
agreed with Channing would have been first to avow
that their prejudice was inveterate, and its consequences sweeping. Such a conviction admitted little
room for liberalism where politics were, directly or
remotely, involved. Literature bordered closely on
politics, and the liberalism of Unitarian Boston was
bounded even in literature by the limits of British
sympathies. Buckminster's Phi Beta Kappa Oration
of 1809 was as emphatic on this point as Channing's
Fast Day Sermon of 1810 was outspoken in its
political antipathies.

" It is our lot," said Buckminster, " to have been born
in an age of tremendous revolution, and the world is
yet covered with the wrecks of its ancient glory, especially of its literary renown. The fury of that storm
which rose in France is passed and spent, but its effects have been felt through the whole system of liberal
education. The foul spirit of innovation and sophistry
has been seen wandering in the very groves of the
Lyceum, and is not yet completely exorcised, though
the spell is broken."

The liberalism of Boston began in a protest against " the foul spirit of innovation," and could hardly begin at any point more advanced. " Infidelity has had one triumph in our days, and we have seen learning as well as virtue trampled under the hoofs of its infuriated steeds, let loose by the hand of impiety." From this attitude of antipathy to innovation, the Unitarian movement began its attempts to innovate, and with astonishing rapidity passed through phases which might well have required ages of growth. In five years Channing began open attack upon the foundation, or what had hitherto been believed the foundation, of the Church ; and from that moment innovation could no longer be regarded as foul.

Of the intellectual movement in all its new directions, Harvard College was the centre. Between 1805 and 1817 the college inspired the worn-out Federalism of Boston with life till then unimagined. Not only did it fill the pulpits with Buckminsters, Channings, and Thachers, whose sermons were an unfailing interest, and whose society was a constant stimulus, but it also maintained a rivalry between the pulpit and the lecture-room. The choice of a new professor was as important and as much discussed as the choice of a new minister. No ordinary political event caused more social interest than the appointment of Henry Ware as Professor of Theology in 1805. In the following year J. Q. Adams was made Professor of Rhetoric, and delivered a course of lectures, which created the school of oratory to which Edward Everett's generation adhered. Four younger men, whose influence was greatly felt in their branches of instruction, received professorships in the next few years, — Jacob Bigelow, who was appointed Professor of Medicine in 1813; Edward Everett, Greek Professor in 1815; John Collins Warren, Professor of Anatomy in the same year; and George Ticknor, Professor of *Belles Lettres* in 1816. In the small society of Boston, a city numbering hardly forty thousand persons, this activity of college and church produced a new era. Where thirty-nine students a year had entered the college before 1800, an average number of sixty-six entered it during the war, and took degrees during the four or five subsequent years. Among them were names familiar to the literature and politics of the next half century. Besides Ticknor and Everett, in 1807 and 1811, Henry Ware graduated in 1812, and his brother William, the author of " Zenobia," in 1816; William Hickling Prescott, in 1814; J. G. Palfrey, in 1815; in 1817, George Bancroft and Caleb Cushing graduated, and Ralph Waldo Emerson entered the college. Boston also drew resources from other quarters, and perhaps showed no stronger proof of its vigor than when, in 1816, it attracted Daniel Webster from New Hampshire to identify himself with the intellect and interests of Massachusetts. Even by reaction the Unitarians stimulated Boston, — as when, a few years afterward, Lyman Beecher accepted the charge of a Boston church in order to resist their encroachments.

The "Anthology," which marked the birth of the new literary school, came in a few years to a natural end, but was revived in 1815 under the name of the "North American Review," by the exertions of William Tudor. The life of the new Review belonged to a later period, and was shaped by other influences than those that surrounded the "Anthology." With the beginning of the next epoch, the provincial stage of the Boston school was closed. More and more its influence tended to become national, and even to affect other countries. Perhaps by a natural consequence rather than by coincidence, the close of the old period was marked by the appearance of a short original poem in the "North American Review" for September, 1817 : —

> "   . . . The hills,
> Rock-ribbed and ancient as the sun ; the vales
> Stretching in pensive quietness between ;
> The venerable woods; the floods that move
> In majesty, and the complaining brooks
> That wind among the meads and make them green, —
> Are but the solemn declarations all,
> Of the great tomb of man.   The golden sun,
> The planets, all the infinite host of heaven
> Are glowing on the sad abodes of death
> Through the still lapse of ages.   All that tread
> The globe are but a handful to the tribes
> That slumber in its bosom.   Take the wings
> Of morning, and the Borean desert pierce;
> Or lose thyself in the continuous woods
> That veil Oregan, where he hears no sound

Save his own dashings, — yet the dead are there ;
And millions in these solitudes, since first
The flight of years began, have laid them down
In their last sleep : the dead reign there alone.
So shalt thou rest : and what if thou shalt fall
Unnoticed by the living, and no friend
Take note of thy departure ?   Thousands more
Will share thy destiny.   The tittering world
Dance to the grave.   The busy brood of care
Plod on, and each one chases as before
His favorite phantom.   Yet all these shall leave
Their mirth and their employments, and shall come
And make their bed with thee."

The appearance of " Thanatopsis " and " Lines to
a Waterfowl" in the early numbers of the " North
American Review," while leaving no doubt that a
new national literature was close at hand, proved also
that it was not to be the product of a single source ;
for Bryant, though greatly tempted to join the Emer-
sons, Channing, Dana, Allston, and Tudor in Boston,
turned finally to New York, where influences of a
different kind surrounded him.   The Unitarian school
could not but take a sober cast, and even its humor
was sure to be tinged with sadness, sarcasm, or irony,
or some serious purpose or passion ; but New York
contained no atmosphere in which such a society
could thrive.   Busy with the charge of practical
work, — the development of industries continually exceeding their power of control, — the people of New
York wanted amusement, and shunned what in
Boston was considered as intellectual.   Their tastes
were gratified by the appearance of a writer whose

first book created a school of literature as distinctly marked as the Unitarian school of Boston, and more decidedly original. "The History of New York, by Diedrich Knickerbocker," appeared in 1809, and stood alone. Other books of the time seemed to recognize some literary parentage. Channing and Buckminster were links in a chain of theologians and preachers. "Thanatopsis" evidently drew inspiration from Wordsworth. Diedrich Knickerbocker owed nothing to any living original.

The "History of New York" was worth more than passing notice. In the development of a national character, as well as of the literature that reflected it, humor was a trait of the utmost interest; and Washington Irving was immediately recognized as a humorist whose name, if he fulfilled the promise of his first attempt, would have a chance of passing into the society of Rabelais, Cervantes, Butler, and Sterne. Few literary tasks were more difficult than to burlesque without vulgarizing, and to satirize without malignity; yet Irving in his first effort succeeded in doing both. The old families, and serious students of colonial history, never quite forgave Irving for throwing an atmosphere of ridicule over the subject of their interest; but Diedrich Knickerbocker's History was so much more entertaining than ordinary histories, that even historians could be excused for regretting that it should not be true.

Yet the book reflected the political passions which marked the period of the Embargo. Besides the burlesque, the " History " contained satire ; and perhaps its most marked trait was the good-nature which, at a time when bitterness was universal in politics, saved Irving's political satire from malignity. Irving meant that no one should mistake the character of the universal genius, Governor Wilhelmus Kieft, surnamed the Testy, who as a youth had made many curious investigations into the nature and operations of windmills, and who came well-nigh being smothered in a slough of unintelligible learning, — " a fearful peril, from the effects of which he never perfectly recovered."

" No sooner had this bustling little man been blown by a whiff of fortune into the seat of government, than he called together his council and delivered a very animated speech on the affairs of the government ; . . . and here he soon worked himself into a fearful rage against the Yankees, whom he compared to the Gauls who desolated Rome, and to the Goths and Vandals who overran the fairest plains of Europe. . . . Having thus artfully wrought up his tale of terror to a climax, he assumed a self-satisfied look, and declared with a nod of knowing import that he had taken measures to put a final stop to these encroachments, — that he had been obliged to have recourse to a dreadful engine of warfare, lately invented, awful in its effects but authorized by direful necessity ; in a word, he was resolved to conquer the Yankees — by Proclamation."

Washington Irving's political relations were those commonly known as Burrite, through his brother Peter, who edited in Burr's interest the " Morning

Chronicle." Antipathy to Jefferson was a natural result, and Irving's satire on the President was the more interesting because the subject offered temptations for ill-tempered sarcasm such as spoiled Federalist humor. The Knickerbocker sketch of Jefferson was worth comparing with Federalist modes of expressing the same ideas : —

"The great defect of Wilhelmus Kieft's policy was that though no man could be more ready to stand forth in an hour of emergency, yet he was so intent upon guarding the national pocket that he suffered the enemy to break its head. . . . All this was a remote consequence of his education at the Hague ; where, having acquired a smattering of knowledge, he was ever a great conner of indexes, continually dipping into books without ever studying to the bottom of any subject, so that he had the scum of all kinds of authors fermenting in his pericranium. In some of these titlepage researches he unluckily stumbled over a grand political *cabalistic word*, which with his customary facility he immediately incorporated into his great scheme of government, to the irretrievable injury and delusion of the honest province of Nieuw Nederlands, and the eternal misleading of all experimental rulers."

Little was wanting to make such a sketch bitter ; but Irving seemed to have the power of deadening venom by a mere trick of hand. Readers of the "History," after a few years had passed, rarely remembered the satire, or supposed that the story contained it. The humor and the style remained to characterize a school.

The originality of the Knickerbocker humor was the more remarkable because it was allowed to stand alone. Irving published nothing else of consequence until 1819, and then, abandoning his early style, inclined to imitate Addison and Steele, although his work was hardly the less original. Irving preceded Walter Scott, whose "Waverley" appeared in 1814, and "Guy Mannering" in 1815; and if either author could be said to influence the other, the influence of Diedrich Knickerbocker on Scott was more evident than that of "Waverley" on Irving.

In the face of the spontaneous burst of genius which at that moment gave to English literature and art a character distinct even in its own experience, Americans might have been excused for making no figure at all. Other periods produced one poet at a time, and measured originality by single poems; or satisfied their ambition by prose or painting of occasional merit. The nineteenth century began in England with genius as plenty as it was usually rare. To Beattie, Cowper, and Burns, succeeded Wordsworth, Coleridge, Scott, Byron, Crabbe, Campbell, Charles Lamb, Moore, Shelley, and Keats. The splendor of this combination threw American and even French talent into the shade, and defied hope of rivalry; but the American mind, as far as it went, showed both freshness and originality. The divergence of American from English standards seemed insignificant to critics who required, as they commonly did, a national literature founded on some new conception, — such as the Shawanee or Aztecs could be supposed to suggest; but to those who expected only a slow variation from European types, the difference was well marked. Channing and Irving were American in literature, as Calhoun and Webster were American in politics. They were the product of influences as peculiar to the country as those which produced Fulton and his steamboat.

While Bryant published "Thanatopsis" and Irving made his studies for the "Sketch-Book," another American of genius perhaps superior to theirs — Washington Allston — was painting in London, before returning to pass the remainder of his life in the neighborhood of Boston and Harvard College. Between thirty and forty years of age, Allston was then in the prime of his powers; and even in a circle of artists which included Turner, Wilkie, Mulready, Constable, Callcott, Crome, Cotman, and a swarm of others equally famous, Allston was distinguished. Other Americans took rank in the same society. Leslie and Stuart Newton were adopted into it, and Copley died only in 1815, while Trumbull painted in London till 1816; but remarkable though they were for the quality of their art, they belonged to a British school, and could be claimed as American only by blood. Allston stood in a relation somewhat different. In part, his apparent Americanism was due to his later return, and to his identification with American society; but the return itself was probably caused

by a peculiar bent of character. His mind was not
wholly English.

Allston's art and his originality were not such
as might have been expected from an American, or
such as Americans were likely to admire ; and the
same might be said of Leslie and Stuart Newton.
Perhaps the strongest instance of all was Edward
Malbone, whose grace of execution was not more
remarkable than his talent for elevating the subject of his exquisite work. So far from sharing the
imagination of Shawanee Indians or even of Democrats, these men instinctively reverted to the most
refined and elevated schools of art. Not only did
Allston show from the beginning of his career a
passion for the nobler standards of his profession,
but also for technical quality, — a taste less usual.
Washington Irving met him in Rome in 1805,
when both were unknown ; and they became warm
friends.

"I do not think I have ever been more captivated on a
first acquaintance," wrote Irving long afterward. "He
was of a light and graceful form, with large blue eyes
and black silken hair. Everything about him bespoke
the man of intellect and refinement. . . . He was ex-
quisitely sensitive to the graceful and the beautiful, and
took great delight in paintings which excelled in color ;
yet he was strongly moved and aroused by objects of
grandeur. I well recollect the admiration with which
he contemplated the sublime statue of Moses, by Michael
Angelo."

The same tastes characterized his life, and gave to his work a distinction that might be Italian, but was certainly not English or usual.

"It was Allston," said Leslie, "who first awakened what little sensibility I may possess to the beauties of color. For long time I took the merit of the Venetians on trust, and if left to myself should have preferred works which I now feel to be comparatively worthless. I remember when the picture of 'The Ages' by Titian was first pointed out to me by Allston as an exquisite work, I thought he was laughing at me." Leslie, if not a great colorist, was seldom incorrect; Stuart Newton had a fine eye for color, and Malbone was emphatically a colorist; but Allston's sensibility to color was rare among artists, and the refinement of his mind was as unusual as the delicacy of his eye.

Allston was also singular in the liberality of his sympathies. "I am by nature, as it respects the arts, a wide liker," he said. In Rome he became acquainted with Coleridge; and the remark of Coleridge which seemed to make most impression on him in their walks "under the pines of the Villa Borghese" was evidently agreeable because it expressed his own feelings. "It was there he taught me this golden rule: never to judge of any work of art by its defects." His admiration for the classics did not prevent him from admiring his contemporaries; his journey through Switzerland not only showed him a

new world of Nature, but also " the truth of Turner's
Swiss scenes, — the poetic truth, — which none before
or since have given." For a young American art-
student in 1804, such sympathies were remarkable;
not so much because they were correct, as because
they were neither American nor English. Neither in
America nor in Europe at that day could art-schools
give to every young man, at the age of twenty-five,
eyes to see the color of Titian, or imagination to feel
the " poetic truth " of Turner.

Other painters, besides those whose names have been
mentioned, were American or worked in America, as
other writers besides Bryant and Irving, and other
preachers besides Buckminster and Channing, were
active in their professions; but for national com-
parisons, types alone serve. In the course of sixteen years certain Americans became distinguished.
Among these, suitable for types, were Calhoun and
Clay in Congress, Pinkney and Webster at the bar,
Buckminster and Channing in the pulpit, Bryant and
Irving in literature, Allston and Malbone in painting.
These men varied greatly in character and qualities.
Some possessed strength, and some showed more
delicacy than vigor; some were humorists, and some
were incapable of a thought that was not serious;
but all were marked by a keen sense of form and
style. So little was this quality expected, that the
world inclined to regard them as un-American because of their refinement. Frenchmen and Italians,
and even Englishmen who knew nothing of America

but its wildness, were disappointed that American oratory should be only a variation from Fox and Burke; that American literature should reproduce Steele and Wordsworth; and that American art should, at its first bound, go back to the ideals of Raphael and Titian. The incongruity was evident. The Americans themselves called persistently for a statesmanship, religion, literature, and art which should be American; and they made a number of experiments to produce what they thought their ideals. In substance they continued to approve nothing which was not marked by style as its chief merit. The oratory of Webster and Calhoun, and even of John Randolph bore the same general and common character of style. The poetry of Bryant, the humor of Irving, the sermons of Channing, and the painting of Allston were the objects of permanent approval to the national mind. Style remained its admiration, even when every newspaper protested against the imitation of outworn forms. Dennie and Jefferson, agreeing in nothing else, agreed in this; the South Carolinian Allston saw color as naturally as the New Englander Bryant heard rhythm; and a people which seemed devoid of sense or standards of beauty, showed more ambition than older societies to acquire both.

Nothing seemed more certain than that the Americans were not artistic, that they had as a people little instinct of beauty; but their intelligence in its higher as in its lower forms was both quick and refined.

Such literature and art as they produced, showed qualities akin to those which produced the swift-sailing schooner, the triumph of naval architecture. If the artistic instinct weakened, the quickness of intelligence increased.

CHAPTER X.

UNTIL 1815 nothing in the future of the American Union was regarded as settled. As late as January, 1815, division into several nationalities was still thought to be possible. Such a destiny, repeating the usual experience of history, was not necessarily more unfortunate than the career of a single nationality wholly American; for if the effects of divided nationality were certain to be unhappy, those of a single society with equal certainty defied experience or sound speculation. One uniform and harmonious system appealed to the imagination as a triumph of human progress, offering prospects of peace and ease, contentment and philanthropy, such as the world had not seen; but it invited dangers, formidable because unusual or altogether unknown. The corruption of such a system might prove to be proportionate with its dimensions, and uniformity might lead to evils as serious as were commonly ascribed to diversity.

The laws of human progress were matter not for dogmatic faith, but for study; and although society instinctively regarded small States, with their clashing interests and incessant wars, as the chief obstacle to improvement, such progress as the world knew had been coupled with those drawbacks. The few examples offered by history of great political societies, relieved from external competition or rivalry, were not commonly thought encouraging. War had been the severest test of political and social character, laying bare whatever was feeble, and calling out whatever was strong; and the effect of removing such a test was an untried problem.

In 1815 for the first time Americans ceased to doubt the path they were to follow. Not only was the unity of their nation established, but its probable divergence from older societies was also well defined. Already in 1817 the difference between Europe and America was decided. In politics the distinction was more evident than in social, religious, literary, or scientific directions; and the result was singular. For a time the aggressions of England and France forced the United States into a path that seemed to lead toward European methods of government; but the popular resistance, or inertia, was so great that the most popular party leaders failed to overcome it, and no sooner did foreign dangers disappear than the system began to revert to American practices; the national government tried to lay aside its assumed powers. When Madison vetoed the bill for internal improvements he could have had no other motive than that of restoring to the government, as far as possible, its original American character.

The result was not easy to understand in theory or to make efficient in practice; but while ·the drift of public opinion, and still more of practical necessity, drew the government slowly toward the European standard of true political sovereignty, nothing showed that the compromise, which must probably serve the public purpose, was to be European in form or feeling. As far as politics supplied a test, the national character had already diverged from any foreign type. Opinions might differ whether the political movement was progressive or retrograde, but in any case the American, in his political character, was a new variety of man.

The social movement was also decided. The war gave a severe shock to the Anglican sympathies of society, and peace seemed to widen the breach between European and American tastes. Interest in Europe languished after Napoleon's overthrow. France ceased to affect American opinion. England became an object of less alarm. Peace produced in the United States a social and economical revolution which greatly curtailed the influence of New England, and with it the social authority of Great Britain. The invention of the steamboat counterbalanced ocean commerce. The South and West gave to society a character more aggressively American than had been known before. That Europe, within certain limits, might tend toward American ideas was possible, but that America should under any circumstances follow the experiences of European development might thenceforward be reckoned as improbable. American character was formed, if not fixed.

The scientific interest of American history centred in national character, and in the workings of a society destined to become vast, in which individuals were important chiefly as types. Although this kind of interest was different from that of European history, it was at least as important to the world. Should history ever become a true science, it must expect to establish its laws, not from the complicated story of rival European nationalities, but from the methodical evolution of a great democracy. North America was the most favorable field on the globe for the spread of a society so large, uniform, and isolated as to answer the purposes of science. There a single homogeneous society could easily attain proportions of three or four hundred million persons, under conditions of undisturbed growth.

In Europe or Asia, except perhaps in China, undisturbed social evolution had been unknown. Without disturbance, evolution seemed to cease. Wherever disturbance occurred, permanence was impossible. Every people in turn adapted itself to the law of necessity. Such a system as that of the United States could hardly have existed for half a century in Europe except under the protection of another power. In the fierce struggle characteristic of European society, systems were permanent in nothing except in the general law, that, whatever other character they might possess they must always be chiefly military.

The want of permanence was not the only or the

most confusing obstacle to the treatment of European history as a science. The intensity of the struggle gave prominence to the individual, until the hero seemed all, society nothing; and what was worse for scientific purposes, the men interested more than the societies. In the dramatic view of history, the hero deserved more to be studied than the community to which he belonged; in truth, he was the society, which existed only to produce him and to perish with him. Against such a view historians were among the last to protest, and protested but faintly when they did so at all. They felt as strongly as their audiences that the highest achievements were alone worth remembering either in history or in art, and that a reiteration of commonplaces was commonplace. With all the advantages of European movement and color, few historians succeeded in enlivening or dignifying the lack of motive, intelligence, and morality, the helplessness characteristic of many long periods in the face of crushing problems, and the futility of human efforts to escape from difficulties religious, political, and social. In a period extending over four or five thousand years, more or less capable of historical treatment, historians were content to illustrate here and there the most dramatic moments of the most striking communities. The hero was their favorite. War was the chief field of heroic action, and even the history of England was chiefly the story of war.

The history of the United States promised to be

free from such disturbances. War counted for little, the hero for less; on the people alone the eye could permanently rest. The steady growth of a vast population without the social distinctions that confused other histories, — without kings, nobles, or armies; without church, traditions, and prejudices, — seemed a subject for the man of science rather than for dramatists or poets. To scientific treatment only one great obstacle existed. Americans, like Europeans, were not disposed to make of their history a mechanical evolution. They felt that they even more than other nations needed the heroic element, because they breathed an atmosphere of peace and industry where heroism could seldom be displayed; and in unconscious protest against their own social conditions they adorned with imaginary qualities scores of supposed leaders, whose only merit was their faculty of reflecting a popular trait. Instinctively they clung to ancient history as though conscious that of all misfortunes that could befall the national character, the greatest would be the loss of the established ideals which alone ennobled human weakness. Without heroes, the national character of the United States had few charms of imagination even to Americans.

Historians and readers maintained Old-World standards. No historian cared to hasten the coming of an epoch when man should study his own history in the same spirit and by the same methods with which he studied the formation of a crystal. Yet history had its scientific as well as its human side, and in American history the scientific interest was greater than the human. Elsewhere the student could study under better conditions the evolution of the individual, but nowhere could he study so well the evolution of a race. The interest of such a subject exceeded that of any other branch of science, for it brought mankind within sight of its own end.

Travellers in Switzerland who stepped across the Rhine where it flowed from its glacier could follow its course among mediæval towns and feudal ruins, until it became a highway for modern industry, and at last arrived at a permanent equilibrium in the ocean. American history followed the same course. With prehistoric glaciers and mediæval feudalism the story had little to do; but from the moment it came within sight of the ocean it acquired interest almost painful. A child could find his way in a river-valley, and a hoy could float on the waters of Holland; but science alone could sound the depths of the ocean, measure its currents, foretell its storms, or fix its relations to the system of Nature. In a democratic ocean science could see something ultimate. Man could go no further. The atom might move, but the general equilibrium could not change.

Whether the scientific or the heroic view were taken, in either case the starting-point was the same, and the chief object of interest was to define national character. Whether the figures of history were treated as heroes or as types, they must be taken to

represent the people.   American types were especially
worth study if they were to represent the greatest
democratic evolution the world could know.   Readers
might judge for themselves what share the individual
possessed in creating or shaping the nation ; but
whether it was small or great, the nation could be
understood only by studying the individual.   For that
reason, in the story of Jefferson and Madison individuals retained their old interest as types of character, if not as sources of power.

In the American character antipathy to war ranked
first among political traits.   The majority of Americans regarded war in a peculiar light, the consequence
of comparative security.   No European nation could
have conducted a war, as the people of America
conducted the War of 1812.   The possibility of doing
so without destruction explained the existence of the
national trait, and assured its continuance.   In politics, the divergence of America from Europe perpet-
uated itself in the popular instinct for peaceable
methods.   The Union took shape originally on the
general lines that divided the civil from the military
elements of the British constitution.   The party of
Jefferson and Gallatin was founded on dislike of
every function of government necessary in a military
system.   Although Jefferson carried his pacific theories to an extreme, and brought about a military reaction, the reactionary movement was neither universal, violent, nor lasting ; and society showed no sign
of changing its convictions.   With greater strength

the country might acquire greater familiarity with warlike methods, but in the same degree was less likely to suffer any general change of habits. Nothing but prolonged intestine contests could convert the population of an entire continent into a race of warriors.

A people whose chief trait was antipathy to war, and to any system organized with military energy, could scarcely develop great results in national administration; yet the Americans prided themselves chiefly on their political capacity. Even the war did not undeceive them, although the incapacity brought into evidence by the war was undisputed, and was most remarkable among the communities which believed themselves to be most gifted with political sagacity. Virginia and Massachusetts by turns admitted failure in dealing with issues so simple that the newest societies, like Tennessee and Ohio, understood them by instinct. That incapacity in national politics should appear as a leading trait in American character was unexpected by Americans, but might naturally result from their conditions. The better test of American character was not political but social, and was to be found not in the government but in the people.

The sixteen years of Jefferson's and Madison's rule furnished international tests of popular intelligence upon which Americans could depend. The ocean was the only open field for competition among nations. Americans enjoyed there no natural or artificial ad-

vantages over Englishmen, Frenchmen, or Spaniards;
indeed, all these countries possessed navies, resources,
and experience greater than were to be found in the
United States.   Yet the Americans developed, in the
course of twenty years, a surprising degree of skill
in naval affairs.   The evidence of their success was
to be found nowhere so complete as in the avowals
of Englishmen who knew best the history of naval
progress.   The American invention of the fast-sailing
schooner or clipper was the more remarkable because,
of all American inventions, this alone sprang from
direct competition with Europe.   During ten centuries
of struggle the nations of Europe had labored to obtain superiority over each other in ship-construction,
yet Americans instantly made improvements which
gave them superiority, and which Europeans were
unable immediately to imitate even after seeing them.
Not only were American vessels better in model,
faster in sailing, easier and quicker in handling, and
more economical in working than the European, but
they were also better equipped.   The English complained as a grievance that the Americans adopted
new and unwarranted devices in naval warfare; that
their vessels were heavier and better constructed, and
their missiles of unusual shape and improper use.
The Americans resorted to expedients that had not
been tried before, and excited a mixture of irritation
and respect in the English service, until Yankee
smartness became a national misdemeanor.

The English admitted themselves to be slow to

change their habits, but the French were both quick and scientific; yet Americans did on the ocean what the French, under stronger inducements, failed to do. The French privateer preyed upon British commerce for twenty years without seriously injuring it; but no sooner did the American privateer sail from French ports, than the rates of insurance doubled in London, and an outcry for protection arose among English shippers which the Admiralty could not calm. The British newspapers were filled with assertions that the American cruiser was the superior of any vessel of its class, and threatened to overthrow England's supremacy on the ocean.

Another test of relative intelligence was furnished by the battles at sea. Instantly after the loss of the "Guerriere" the English discovered and complained that American gunnery was superior to their own. They explained their inferiority by the length of time that had elapsed since their navy had found on the ocean an enemy to fight. Every vestige of hostile fleets had been swept away, until, after the battle of Trafalgar, British frigates ceased practice with their guns. Doubtless the British navy had become somewhat careless in the absence of a dangerous enemy, but Englishmen were themselves aware that some other cause must have affected their losses. Nothing showed that Nelson's line-of-battle ships, frigates, or sloops were as a rule better fought than the "Macedonian" and "Java," the "Avon" and "Reindeer." Sir Howard Douglas, the chief authority on the subject, attempted in vain to explain British reverses by the deterioration of British gunnery. His analysis showed only that American gunnery was extraordinarily good. Of all vessels, the sloop-of-war, — on account of its smallness, its quick motion, and its more accurate armament of thirty-two-pound carronades,— offered the best test of relative gunnery, and Sir Howard Douglas in commenting upon the destruction of the " Peacock " and " Avon " could only say, —

" In these two actions it is clear that the fire of the British vessels was thrown too high, and that the ordnance of their opponents were expressly and carefully aimed at and took effect chiefly in the hull."

The battle of the " Hornet " and " Penguin " as well as those of the " Reindeer " and " Avon," showed that the excellence of American gunnery continued till the close of the war. Whether at point-blank range or at long-distance practice, the Americans used guns as they had never been used at sea before.

None of the reports of former British victories showed that the British fire had been more destructive at any previous time than in 1812, and no report of any commander since the British navy existed showed so much damage inflicted on an opponent in so short a time as was proved to have been inflicted on themselves by the reports of British commanders in the American war. The strongest proof of American superiority was given by the best British officers, like Broke, who strained every nerve to maintain an equality with American gunnery. So instantaneous and energetic was the effort that, according to the British historian of the war, " a British forty-six-gun frigate of 1813 was half as effective again as a British forty-six-gun frigate of 1812 ; " and, as he justly said, " the slaughtered crews and the shattered hulks " of the captured British ships proved that no want of their old fighting qualities accounted for their repeated and almost habitual mortifications.[1]

Unwilling as the English were to admit the superior skill of Americans on the ocean, they did not hesitate to admit it, in certain respects, on land. The American rifle in American hands was affirmed to have no equal in the world. This admission could scarcely be withheld after the lists of killed and wounded which followed almost every battle ; but the admission served to check a wider inquiry. In truth, the rifle played but a small part in the war. Winchester's men at the river Raisin may have owed their over-confidence, as the British Forty-first owed its losses, to that weapon, and at New Orleans five or six hundred of Coffee's men, who were out of range, were armed with the rifle ; but the surprising losses of the British were commonly due to artillery and musketry fire. At New Orleans the artillery was chiefly engaged. The artillery battle of January 1, according to British accounts, amply proved the superiority of American gunnery on that occasion, which was probably the fairest test during the war.

[1] James, pp. 525, 528. .

The battle of January 8 was also chiefly an artillery battle; the main British column never arrived within fair musket range; Pakenham was killed by a grape-shot, and the main column of his troops halted more than one hundred yards from the parapet.

The best test of British and American military qualities, both for men and weapons, was Scott's battle of Chippawa. Nothing intervened to throw a doubt over the fairness of the trial. Two parallel lines of regular soldiers, practically equal in numbers, armed with similar weapons, moved in close order toward each other, across a wide open plain, without cover or advantage of position, stopping at intervals to load and fire, until one line broke and retired. At the same time two three-gun batteries, the British being the heavier, maintained a steady fire from positions opposite each other. According to the reports, the two infantry lines in the centre never came nearer than eighty yards. Major-General Riall reported that then, owing to severe losses, his troops broke and could not be rallied. Comparison of the official reports showed that the British lost in killed and wounded four hundred and sixty-nine men; the Americans, two hundred and ninety-six. Some doubts always affect the returns of wounded, because the severity of the wound cannot be known; but dead men tell their own tale. Riall reported one hundred and forty-eight killed; Scott reported sixty-one. The severity of the losses showed that the battle was sharply contested, and proved the personal bravery of both armies.   Marksmanship decided the result, and the returns proved that the American fire was superior to that of the British in the proportion of more than fifty per cent if estimated by the entire loss, and of two hundred and forty-two to one hundred if estimated by the deaths alone.

The conclusion seemed incredible, but it was supported by the results of the naval battles.   The Americans showed superiority amounting in some cases to twice the efficiency of their enemies in the use of weapons.   The best French critic of the naval war, Jurien de la Gravière said : " An enormous superiority in the rapidity and precision of their fire can alone explain the difference in the losses sustained by the combatants." [1]   So far from denying this conclusion the British press constantly alleged it, and the British officers complained of it.   The discovery caused great surprise, and in both British services much attention was at once directed to improvement in artillery and musketry.   Nothing could exceed the frankness with which Englishmen avowed their inferiority.   According to Sir Francis Head, " gunnery was in naval warfare in the extraordinary state of ignorance we have just described, when our lean children, the American people, taught us, rod in hand, our first lesson in the art."   The English text-book on Naval Gunnery, written by Major-General Sir Howard Douglas immediately after the peace, devoted more attention to the short American war

[1] Guerres Maritimes, ii. 286, 287.

than to all the battles of Napoleon, and began by
admitting that Great Britain had " entered with too
great confidence on war with a marine much more
expert than that of any of our European enemies."
The admission appeared " objectionable " even to
the author ; [1] but he did not add, what was equally
true, that it applied as well to the land as to the
sea service.

No one questioned the bravery of the British forces,
or the ease with which they often routed larger
bodies of militia ; but the losses they inflicted were
rarely as great as those they suffered.   Even at
Bladensburg, where they met little resistance, their
loss was several times greater than that of the
Americans.   At Plattsburg, where the intelligence
and quickness of Macdonough and his men alone won
the victory, his ships were in effect stationary batteries, and enjoyed the same superiority in gunnery.
" The ' Saratoga,' " said his official report, " had fifty-
five round-shot in her hull ; the ' Confiance,' one
hundred and five.   The enemy's shot passed principally just over our heads, as there were not twenty
whole hammocks in the nettings at the close of the
action."

The greater skill of the Americans was not due to
special training, for the British service was better
trained in gunnery, as in everything else, than the
motley armies and fleets that fought at New Orleans
and on the Lakes.   Critics constantly said that every

[1] Naval Gunnery (Second edition), p. 3.

American had learned from his childhood the use of the rifle, but he certainly had not learned to use cannon in shooting birds or hunting deer, and he knew less than the Englishman about the handling of artillery and muskets. The same intelligence that selected the rifle and the long pivot-gun for favorite weapons was shown in handling the carronade, and every other instrument however clumsy.

Another significant result of the war was the sudden development of scientific engineering in the United States. This branch of the military service owed its efficiency and almost its existence to the military school at West Point, established in 1802. The school was at first much neglected by government. The number of graduates before the year 1812 was very small; but at the outbreak of the war the corps of engineers was already efficient. Its chief was Colonel Joseph Gardner Swift, of Massachusetts, the first graduate of the academy: Colonel Swift planned the defences of New York harbor. The lieutenant-colonel in 1812 was Walker Keith Armistead, of Virginia, — the third graduate, who planned the defences of Norfolk. Major William McRee, of North Carolina, became chief engineer to General Brown, and constructed the fortifications at Fort Erie, which cost the British General Gordon Drummond the loss of half his army, besides the mortification of defeat. Captain Eleazer Derby Wood, of New York, constructed Fort Meigs, which enabled Harrison to defeat the attack of Proctor in May,

1813.   Captain Joseph Gilbert Totten, of New York,
was chief engineer to General Izard at Plattsburg,
where he directed the fortifications that stopped the
advance of Prevost's great army.   None of the works
constructed by a graduate of West Point was captured by the enemy; and had an engineer been employed at Washington by Armstrong and Winder,
the city would have been easily saved.

Perhaps without exaggeration the West Point
Academy might be said to have decided, next to the
navy, the result of the war.   The works at New
Orleans were simple in character, and as far as they
were due to engineering skill were directed by Major
Latour, a Frenchman; but the war was already ended
when the battle of New Orleans was fought.   During
the critical campaign of 1814, the West Point engineers doubled the capacity of the little American
army for resistance, and introduced a new and scientific character into American life.

In the application of science the steamboat was the
most striking success; but Fulton's invention, however useful, was neither the most original nor the
most ingenious of American efforts, nor did it offer
the best example of popular characteristics.   Perhaps Fulton's torpedo and Stevens's screw-propeller
showed more originality than was proved by the
" Clermont."   The fast-sailing schooner with its pivot-
gun — an invention that grew out of the common
stock of nautical intelligence — best illustrated the
character of the people.

That the individual should rise to a higher order either of intelligence or morality than had existed in former ages was not to be expected, for the United States offered less field for the development of individuality than had been offered by older and smaller societies. The chief function of the American Union was to raise the average standard of popular intelligence and well-being, and at the close of the War of 1812 the superior average intelligence of Americans was so far admitted that Yankee acuteness, or smartness, became a national reproach; but much doubt remained whether the intelligence belonged to a high order, or proved a high morality. From the earliest ages, shrewdness was associated with unscrupulousness; and Americans were freely charged with wanting honesty. The charge could neither be proved nor disproved. American morality was such as suited a people so endowed, and was high when compared with the morality of many older societies; but, like American intelligence, it discouraged excess. Probably the political morality shown by the government and by public men during the first sixteen years of the century offered a fair gauge of social morality. Like the character of the popular inventions, the character of the morals corresponded to the wants of a growing democratic society; but time alone could decide whether it would result in a high or a low national ideal.

Finer analysis showed other signs of divergence from ordinary standards. If Englishmen took pride

in one trait more than in another, it was in the
steady uniformity of their progress. The innovating
and revolutionary quality of the French mind irritated them. America showed an un-English rapidity
in movement. In politics, the American people between 1787 and 1817 accepted greater changes than
had been known in England since 1688. In religion, the Unitarian movement of Boston and Harvard
College would never have been possible in England,
where the defection of Oxford or Cambridge, and the
best educated society in the United Kingdom, would
have shaken Church and State to their foundations.
In literature the American school was chiefly remarkable for the rapidity with which it matured. The
first book of Irving was a successful burlesque of
his own ancestral history ; the first poem of Bryant
sang of the earth only as a universal tomb ; the
first preaching of Channing assumed to overthrow the
Trinity ; and the first paintings of Allston aspired to
recover the ideal perfection of Raphael and Titian.
In all these directions the American mind showed
tendencies that surprised Englishmen more than they
struck Americans. Allston defended himself from
the criticism of friends who made complaint of his
return to America. He found there, as he maintained, not only a growing taste for art, but " a
quicker appreciation " of artistic effort than in
any European land. If the highest intelligence of
American society were to move with such rapidity, the time could not be far distant when it would

pass into regions which England never liked to contemplate.

Another intellectual trait, as has been already noticed, was the disposition to relax severity. Between the theology of Jonathan Edwards and that of William Ellery Channing was an enormous gap, not only in doctrines but also in methods. Whatever might be thought of the conclusions reached by Edwards and Hopkins, the force of their reasoning commanded respect. Not often had a more strenuous effort than theirs been made to ascertain God's will, and to follow it without regard to weaknesses of the flesh. The idea that the nature of God's attributes was to be preached only as subordinate to the improvement of man, agreed little with the spirit of their religion. The Unitarian and Universalist movements marked the beginning of an epoch when ethical and humanitarian ideas took the place of metaphysics, and even New England turned from contemplating the omnipotence of the Deity in order to praise the perfections of his creatures.

The spread of great popular sects like the Universalists and Campbellites, founded on assumptions such as no Orthodox theology could tolerate, showed a growing tendency to relaxation of thought in that direction. The struggle for existence was already mitigated, and the first effect of the change was seen in the increasing cheerfulness of religion. Only when men found their actual world almost a heaven, could they lose overpowering anxiety about the world to

come. Life had taken a softer aspect, and as a consequence God was no longer terrible. Even the
wicked became less mischievous in an atmosphere
where virtue was easier than vice. Punishments
seemed mild in a society where every offender could
cast off his past, and create a new career. For the
first time in history, great bodies of men turned away
from their old religion, giving no better reason than
that it required them to believe in a cruel Deity, and
rejected necessary conclusions of theology because
they were inconsistent with human self-esteem.

The same optimism marked the political movement.
Society was weary of strife, and settled gladly into
a political system which left every disputed point
undetermined. The public seemed obstinate only
in believing that all was for the best, as far as the
United States were concerned, in the affairs of mankind. The contrast was great between this temper
of mind and that in which the Constitution had been
framed ; but it was no greater than the contrast
in the religious opinions of the two periods, while
the same reaction against severity marked the new
literature. The rapid accumulation of wealth and
increase in physical comfort told the same story
from the standpoint of economy. On every side
society showed that ease was for a time to take
the place of severity, and enjoyment was to have
its full share in the future national existence.

The traits of intelligence, rapidity, and mildness
seemed fixed in the national character as early as

1817, and were likely to become more marked as time should pass. A vast amount of conservatism still lingered among the people; but the future spirit of society could hardly fail to be intelligent, rapid in movement, and mild in method. Only in the distant future could serious change occur, and even then no return to European characteristics seemed likely. The American continent was happier in its conditions and easier in its resources than the regions of Europe and Asia, where Nature revelled in diversity and conflict. If at any time American character should change, it might as probably become sluggish as revert to the violence and extravagances of Old-World development. The inertia of several hundred million people, all formed in a similar social mould, was as likely to stifle energy as to stimulate evolution.

With the establishment of these conclusions, a new episode in American history began in 1815. New subjects demanded new treatment, no longer dramatic but steadily tending to become scientific. The traits of American character were fixed; the rate of physical and economical growth was established; and history, certain that at a given distance of time the Union would contain so many millions of people, with wealth valued at so many millions of dollars, became thenceforward chiefly concerned to know what kind of people these millions were to be. They were intelligent, but what paths would their intelligence select? They were quick, but what solution of insoluble problems would quickness hurry ? They were scientific, and what control would their science exercise over their destiny ? They were mild, but what corruptions would their relaxations bring ? They were peaceful, but by what machinery were their corruptions to be purged ? What interests were to vivify a society so vast and uniform ? What ideals were to ennoble it ? What object, besides physical content, must a democratic continent aspire to attain ? For the treatment of such questions, history required another century of experience.

GENERAL LIST OF MAPS AND PLANS.

VOLUME VIII.

GENERAL INDEX.

tures, 138; chief author of the Kentucky Resolutions, 140 *et seq* , leader of the Virginia school, 143; characteristics of, 144 *et seq.* ; his political doctrines, 146 *et seq.*, 156 ; Thomas Moore's verses on, 167: visionary, 170; his ideas of progress, 178, 179; personal characteristics, 185 *et seq.* ; his dress, 187; ii. 366, 405; social preeminence, i. 188; his inauguration, 191; his antipathy to Marshall, 192, 194; purity of his life, 196; his Inaugural Address, 199 *et seq.* ; his conception of government, 210 *et seq.* ; his foreign policy, 214 *et seq.* ; his Cabinet. 218 *et seq.* ; his plans for the navy, 222 *et seq.* ; his treatment of patronage, 224, 294; his New Haven letter, 226; his first annual message, 248; his course with regard to the Judiciary, 255 *et seq.* ; his abnegation of power, 262; his power, 266; his theory of internal politics, 272; contradictions in his character, 277; his hopefulness, 307 *et seq.* ; as a man of science, 310; his dislike for New Englanders. 310 *et seq.* ; his letter to Paine, 316; attacked by Callender, 322: sensitiveness of. 324; his relations with Callender, 325 *et seq.* ; sends Lear to St. Domingo, 389 ; ignorant of Bonaparte's schemes, 403 *et seq.*; his eyes opened, 409; his letter to Dupont de Nemours, 410; writes to Livingston defining his position with respect to France and Spain, 424; his annual message, 1802, 427 ; ignores the war party, 428 ; replies to their demand for papers touching the right of deposit at New Orleans, 430; quiets the West, 432; attempts the purchase of New Orleans, 432 *et seq.* ; his language to Thornton, 436; prefers Natchez

to New Orleans as a seat of trade, 443; his apparent inconsistency, 443 *et seq.* ; the essence of his statesmanship, 445; proposes alliance with England, ii. 1, 78; instructs Pinckney to offer a consideration to Spain for New Orleans and Florida, 22; writes a defence of his use of patronage for the Boston "Chronicle," 82; his amendment to the Constitution regarding Louisiana, 83; his letter to Breckinridge on the subject, 84; to Paine, 86; draws up a new amendment, 86; his reply to W. C. Nicholas, 89; his message Oct. 7, 1803, 92; his bill for the administration of Louisiana, 119; his view of the Louisiana treaty and legislation, 130; requests Congress to enlarge the Mediterranean force, 140; interview with Burr, 175; declines to appoint Burr to an executive office, 176; his knowledge of Federalist schemes, 192; his confidence in his popularity, 202; receives the electoral votes of Massachusetts and New Hampshire, 204: his message November, 1804, 206 ; his disappointment at the acquittal of Justice Chase, 243; his authority in foreign affairs, 245; desires to obtain West Florida, 245; explains to Senator Breckinridge his course toward Spain, 248; his plan to obtain West Florida, 249; instructs Monroe with regard to the Spanish claims, 250; the harvest season of his life, 252; sends troops to Natchez, 254; makes no demand for West Florida when Louisiana is delivered, 256; declares Mobile within the United States, 263; entertains Yrujo at Monticello, 266; his conviction of the power of American commercial interests,

campaign, 265; his remarks in August, 1812, on the Canadian campaign, 337; re-elected President, 413; wishes Monroe to command western army, 419, 420, 425; his annual message of 1812, 430–433; his "fair calculation" on Napoleon's success, vii. 2; his message on British "demoralizing and disorganizing contrivances," 31, 32; his second Inaugural Address, 33; his relations toward Gallatin and Monroe, 39; consents to Gallatin's departure, 42, 43; his annual message, May 25, 1813, 53, 54; dangerous illness of, 55, 58; his reply to the Senate in regard to Gallatin's absence, 59, 60; his skill in overthrowing an enemy, 64; goes to Montpelier, 70; his annual message of Dec. 7, 1813, 365, 366; his embargo message of Dec. 9, 1813, 367, 368, 372, 392; accepts Castlereagh's offer of direct negotiation, 371; nominates commissioners and a Secretary of the Treasury, 371; his obstinacy, 372, 393; abandons system of commercial restrictions, 373, 374, 379; causes of his abandonment of commercial restrictions, 373, 374, 377, 394, 395; his language about Napoleon, 392; appoints G. W. Campbell Secretary of the Treasury, 396, 397; appoints Richard Rush attorney-general, 398; appoints R. J. Meigs postmaster-general, 401; overcomes his party enemies, 402; his dislike of Armstrong, 405, 406, 414; offended by Armstrong's letter appointing Andrew Jackson a major-general, 410, 411; his court-martial on William Hull, 415–417; his mode of resisting usurpations on State rights, viii. 8; irritated by Armstrong's neglect to defend Washington, 121; calls a cabinet meeting, June 23, 1814, 121; selects General Winder to command at Washington, 122; calls for militia, 131, 132; reviews the army at the Old Fields, 134; goes to Winder's headquarters at eight o'clock on the morning of August 24, 137; arrives on the battle-field at Bladensburg, 140; his movements, August 24–27, 149–151, 156, 157, 300; ix. 21; charges Monroe with the war department in Armstrong's absence, viii. 158; his interview with Armstrong, August 29, 160, 161; greatly shaken by the capture of Washington, 160, 230, 231; appoints Monroe Secretary of War, 163; his unpopularity, 229, 230; his disappointments, 237, 238; his annual message of Sept. 20, 1814, 239, 240; vetoes bill for incorporating a national bank, 260; to be coerced into retiring, 306, 309; ix. 3, 4; characterized by the Londo̅ press, ix. 2–6; decides to omit impressment from treaty, 33; Lord Liverpool's remark on, 36; sends treaty of peace to the Senate, 58 recommends preparation for war. 82, 83; his annual message of 1815, 105, 106; his annual message of 1816, 143, 144; his veto of internal improvements, 151, 169, 192, 220; his retirement, 153.

Maguaga, battle of, vi. 325.

"Maidstone," 36-gun British frigate, vii. 266.

Mail routes in 1800, i. 15; in 1816, ix. 170, 171.

Maine, District of, a part of Massachusetts, i. 20; boundary of, disputed, ii. 358, 383, 392; viii. 4, 94, 95; two counties of, occupied by British expedition in 1814, viii. 95, 96, 267, 272; ix. 17; portion of, demanded by Great Britain, viii. 268, 287; concessions proposed by Gov-

report of legislature on a New England Convention, Feb. 18,1814, 8; election in April, 1814, 9–11, 13; prosperity in 1814, 14; expressions of clergy, 20–23; regular troops in, vii. 284; viii. 95, 316; territory of, occupied, 95, 96; object of, in dependence on militia, 220; places militia under State major-general, 221, ix. 160; "dangerous and perplexing" situation of, viii. 222–224; calls a New England Convention at Hartford, 225–227, 287; election of November, 1814, a federalist triumph, 228, 288, 289; Jefferson's remark that Virginia got no aid from, 233; money furnished by, 233–235; men furnished by, 235, 236; moral support furnished by, 236, 237; arrears of internal taxes in, 255, 256; legislature of, refuses to co-operate in expelling enemy from Maine, 272, 304; creates a State army of ten thousand men, 272, 282; her delegation to the Hartford Convention, 290–292; accepts the report of the Hartford Convention, 295, 301; banks refuse to lend money to the State, 302; suspends organization of State army, 303; disunion sentiment of, 305–308; her indifference to the negotiation at Ghent, ix. 16, 45; alone interested in the obstacles to a treaty, 49; election of April, 1815, 92; interests affected by peace, 95, 97; suffers from Dallas's arrangements, 98–103; election of April, 1816, 133; legislature denounces Compensation Act, 137; in Presidential election of 1816, 139.

Massassinway, council at, vi. 111.

"Matilda," privateer, captured, vii. 330.

Mat hews, George, appointed commissioner to take possession of East Florida, vi. 237; his proceedings, 238–240; disavowed, 240–242.

McArthur, Duncan, colonel of Ohio militia, vi. 298, 326, 328, 332, 334; brigadier-general, vii. 128.

McClure, George, brigadier-general of New York militia, commands at Niagara, vii. 200; evacuates Fort George and burns Newark, 201, 202.

McDonald, William, captain in Nineteenth U. S. Infantry, on Ripley's staff, his account of the battle of Lundy's Lane, viii. 55, 57.

McDonogh, P., lieutenant of artillery in Fort Erie, viii. 76.

McFarland, D., major of Twenty-third U. S. Infantry, viii. 35; at Chippawa, 42; at Lundy's Lane, 50; wounded, 52, 63.

McKean, Thomas, Governor of Pennsylvania, i. 228; iii. 210; declines to remove Judge Brackenridge, ii. 196, 259.

McKee, John, vi. 237.

McLean, John, member of Congress from Ohio, ix. 107.

McQueen, Peter, half-breed Creek Indian, visits Pensacola, vii. 228; attacked at Burnt Corn, 229; captures Fort Mims, 229–231; claims forty-eight hundred gun-men, 233; escapes to Florida, 257.

McRae, Alexander, counsel for Burr, iii. 445.

McRee, William, major of engineers, advises Brown to move against Riall, viii. 47; directs entrenchments at Fort Erie, 67, 76; ix. 235.

Meade, lieutenant of the British frigate "Leopard," iv. 12.

Meade, Cowles, governor of Mississippi Territory, iii. 304; arrests Burr, 326.

Meade, William, bishop of Virginia, i. 193.

Mecklenburg, Grand Duchy of, closes

asking for two assistant Secretaries of War, 206; of June 1, 1812, recommending a declaration of war with England, 221–226; annual, of Nov. 4, 1812, 430–433; special, of Feb. 24, 1813, on British licenses of trade with New England, vii. 31, 32; annual of May 25, 1813, 53, 54; annual of Dec. 7, 1813, 365; ix. 5; special of Dec. 9, 1813, asking for an embargo, vii. 367, 368, 372; special of March 31, 1814, recommending abandonment of commercial restrictions, 373, 374; annual of Sept. 20, 1814, viii. 239; veto, of Jan. 30, 1815, on the bill to incorporate the United States Bank, 260; special, of Feb. 20, 1815, transmitting treaty of peace, ix. 82; annual, of Dec. 5, 1815, 105; annual, of Dec. 3, 1816, 143, 144; special, of March 3, 1817, vetoing bill for internal improvements, 151.

"Messenger," stallion, i. 51.

Mexico, Jefferson's language to, iv. 340, 341.

Michigan Territory, iii. 176; population in 1810, v. 289. (See Detroit.)

Michillimackinaw, Island of, vi. 294; captured by British expedition, 314, 320; Croghan's expedition against, viii. 32; demanded by British at Ghent, ix. 34.

Milan Decree (see Decrees).

Militia, condition of, in 1808, iv. 210, 213; appropriation for, 224; constitutional power of Congress over, vi. 159, 160, 400; Cheves's opinion on the war power, 160; act authorizing call for one hundred thousand, 204, 390; refuses to cross the frontier, 351, 352, 360; of Kentucky, 391, 393 (see Kentucky, Tennessee, Georgia, Washington City); praised by political parties, viii. 217; system a failure in 1814,

217–219; tainted with fraud, 219; intended for overthrowing the national government, 220; of Massachusetts and Connecticut withdrawn from national service in September, 1814, 220, **221**; of Vermont refused for defence of Plattsburg, 222; views of the Massachusetts Senate regarding, 226; Monroe's complaints of, 264; Monroe's scheme for drafting from, 265, 266; Giles's bill for raising eighty thousand by draft, 269–280; Troup's opinion of, 274; Madison's recommendation for, ix. 105.

Mill, James, his reply to Spence and Cobbett, iv. 329.

Milledge, John, Governor of Georgia, and the Yazoo sale, i. 305.

Miller, James, lieutenant-colonel of Fourth U. S. Infantry, at Detroit, vi. 326, 328; appointed colonel of the Twenty-first Infantry, viii. 36; at Lundy's Lane, captures the British guns, 54, 55, 60; promoted to brigadier, takes command of Scott's brigade, 87; carries British battery in sortie from Fort Erie, 87, 88.

Miller, John, colonel of Nineteenth U. S. Infantry, leads sortie at Fort Meigs, vii. 107.

Miller, Morris S., member of Congress from New York, on the States taking care of themselves in 1814, viii. 276.

Miller, Samuel, captain of marines, at Bladensburg, viii. 143.

Minor of Natchez, iii. 224, 225, 315.

Mint, opposition to, i. 299; ii. 77.

Miranda, Francesco de, his plans to revolutionize Colombia, iii. 189 *et seq.*; distrusted by Burr, 189, 238; visits Washington, 190; his letter to Madison, 191; sails, 191; defeated by the Spaniards, 209; returns to New York, 238.

390; his explanations to the British Government, 391; his letter to Louverture, 392, 393; his instructions to Leclerc, 397, 398; orders the occupation of Louisiana, 399 400; attempts to obtain Florida, 402; Jefferson's messages to, 404, 410, 411, 413, 443; his account of his miscarriage at St. Domingo, 416; fears a war with the United States, ii. 2; abandons his colonial system, 14 *et seq.*; scene with Lord Whitworth, 19; reveals his determination to cede Louisiana, 25-28; angry scene with his brothers, 34 *et seq.*; his *projet* of a secret convention respecting Louisiana, 40; objects to the payment of claims, 51; his inducement to sell Louisiana, 52, his conduct toward Spain, 56; his avowal as to the sale of Louisiana, 61; his reasons for betraying Charles IV., 63; for selling Louisiana, 63 *et seq.*, repudiates drafts on the public Treasury, 270; prepares for a descent on England, 291; weary of Talleyrand, 310, 312; Jefferson's language about, 348, 353, 381; his irritation at Jerome's marriage, 379; his intervention in Monroe's Spanish negotiation, iii. 26, 29, 30, 32, 41, 82; not influenced by corruption of his subordinates, 42; begins war with Austria and Russia, 73, 76, 77, 103; forbids trade with St. Domingo, 89; captures Ulm and enters Vienna, 106, 370; returns to Paris, 371; his financial measures in 1806, 372-375; defeats Talleyrand's plan for a settlement between Spain and the United States, 383; wins the battle of Jena, 388; issues the Decree of Berlin, 389; makes the treaty of Tilsit, iv. 62, 105; attacks Portugal and Denmark, 106, enforces his Berlin Decree against

the United States, 109. 110; Armstrong's story about his attitude toward Florida, 114; orders his armies into Spain, 117; his proposed division of Portugal, 119; offers Lucien the crown of Spain, 124; issues the Decree of Milan, 126; treats the United States as at war with England, 221, 292, 295, 312; seizes the Spanish Court, 298; crowns Joseph King of Spain, 300; his Spanish plan for conquering England, 303. issues the Bayonne Decree, 304; his Spanish campaign, v. 22-28; his severity toward American commerce, 30-32; withholds Florida, 32, 33; his causes for rupture with the United States, 39, 40; his war with Austria in 1809, 106, 134; learns the repeal of the embargo and of the British Orders, 136; his first reply to Armstrong's communication, 137, drafts decree withdrawing the Milan Decree, 139; cause of his hesitation, 140, 141; lays aside his repealing decree, 141; his view of the right of search, 137, 145, 149; his draft of Vienna Decree of Aug. 4, 1809, 143, 144, 230, 233, 236; quarrels with his brother Louis, 146, 147; his increased severity toward the United States, 150-152, 220; calls a Cabinet council on commerce, Dec. 19 1809, 220, 221; discussions with Montalivet, 221, 223; his note to Gaudin on American ships, 224; his want of money, 225, 226, 237; calls for a report from Champagny, Jan 10, 1810, 226, 227; his dislike for Armstrong, 228, 229; his condition for the revocation of his decrees, 229; his draft of note asserting retaliation on the Non-intercourse Act, 230, 231; his reply to Armstrong's remonstrances, 234, 235; his memory,

235 ; his Decree of Rambouillet, 236 ; his threats of annexing Holland, 238, 246; his annexation of Holland, 241, 242; his reflections on Macon's act, 244, 245; his license system, 246 ; his instructions to Champagny ordering announcement that the decrees will be withdrawn, 253; dictates letter of Aug. 5, 1810, 253; his idea of a trap, 257, 383: his instructions of Dec. 13, 1810, on the non-intercourse and the Floridas, 384 ; on commercial liberties, 386 ; his address of March 17. 1811, to the deputies of the Hanse Towns, 396, 397, his address of March 24, 1811, to the Paris merchants, 398 399, 420; appoints Maret in place of Champagny, 401 ; orders a report on American commerce, 402, 403 ; admits American cargoes, May 4, 1811, 404; his instruction of Aug. 28, 1811, about Spanish America and Florida, 407, 408: his rupture with Russia and Sweden, 408–427 , his order of May 4, 1811, opening his ports to American commerce, vi. 44, 59 ; probable amount of his spoliations, 247; his restrictions on American commerce, 247; goes to Holland, Sept. 19, 1811, 248; his interview with Joel Barlow, 249 ; his extension of the license system in January. 1812, 250 ; his seizure of Swedish Pomerania, 251, 252 ; his Decree of St. Cloud, April 28, 1811, 255, 256; his departure for Poland, May 9. 1812, 258 ; enters Russia, 259, 288; his battle at Borodino, Sept. 7, 1812, 263 ; enters Moscow, Sept. 15, 1812, 263; begins his retreat. 264 ; his passage of the Beresina, 264 ; his return to Paris, December, 1812. 265 ; enters Moscow, vii. 4, 26, 27; begins retreat, 9 ; leaves his army, 11 ; re-

turns to Paris, 30; organizes a new army, 339; wins battles of Lützen and Bautzen, 340, 344, 391; makes armistice, 340, wins battle at Dresden, 350; overthrown at Leipzig, 355, 360, 370, 393 : approaching fall of, 362, 393: effects of overthrow on Congress and the President, 393–395 his return from Elba, ix. 56, 83: overthrown at Waterloo, 104.

"Narcissus," British 32-gun frigate. captures " Viper," vii. 313.

Nash, Thomas, ii. 333.

Natchez delivered to the United States, i. 355.

"National Intelligencer," origin of, i. 121; publishes Paine's letters, 328 ; prints the British Impressment Proclamation, iv. 166, 172, 186; publishes the Milan Decree, 195 ; on renewal of intercourse with Great Britain, v. 75; on Erskine's disavowal, 109. 110: Joel Barlow's letter in, 299; office destroyed by Cockburn, viii. 147.

Naturalization, the law of, in England and America, ii. 337 et seq ; British laws of, vii. 21-23; issue raised, 360

Naturalization law adopted, i. 301.

"Nautilus," East India Company's cruiser, ix 73.

"Nautilus." sloop-of-war captured, vi. 369 386; vii. 312. 313.

Navigation, British law of. ii. 318, 321, 413

Navigation Act. moved by Macon, v. 183.

Navigation Act of 1816. ix. 146, 147.

Navy, British, cost and pay-roll of, vii. 20.

Navy Department (see Samuel Smith, Robert Smith, Paul Hamilton, William Jones, B. W. Crowninshield).

Navy of the United States, Jeffer-

ate "Leopard," iv. 1–30; nature of reparation demanded for, 31, 39, 45, 46, 62 (see "Chesapeake" affair); the United States in 1807 almost the only, 66; West India report on trade of, 67–69; British lawyers on violations of law of, 77; Spencer Perceval's Orders in Council restricting rights of, 79–104 (see Orders in Council); Napoleon's Milan Decree, making war on, 126 (see Decrees); British disregard of law of, in America, 136, 137; Napoleon's idea of, as exempt from interference, v. 137, 149; list of restrictions on commerce of, 152; of 1809, 165; Napoleon's declaration that, after the Milan Decree, there were no more, 227 (see Napoleon); defence of, by Russia and Sweden, 409–428 (see Impressment, Licenses, Spoliations); Madison's indifference to duties of, in West Florida, 309, 310 (see Florida, East and West); Act of 1816, to preserve relations of, ix. 147.

Newark, on the Niagara River, burned by McClure, vii. 202.

Newbury, memorial of town-meeting in January, 1814, viii. 6.

Newburyport town-meeting in January, 1809, iv. 410.

New England in 1800, i. 18; schoolhouses, 19; population, 20; poverty, 21; commerce and manufactures, 21 et seq.; social system, 76; schools, 76; society, organization of, 108, temper of, toward Jefferson in 1802, 308–330; conspiracy of 1804 in, ii. 160–190, 391, 392; its conservatism, Jefferson's second Inaugural on, iii. 5–9; townships, Jefferson's opinion of, iv. 441; prosperity of shipping in, 1807–1810, v. 15; prosperity of manufactures in, 16–21; encouragement

of manufactures in, 196, 197; F. J. Jackson's reception in, 213–217; refuses to take the war loan of 1812, vi. 207; favored by British government in the war, vii. 31, 32; furnishes money and supplies to Canada, 146, 367. 368; benefited by the British blockade, 264, 283, 367; military force assigned to, 284; banks, their condition and influence, 387, 389; viii. 15; blockaded, April 25, 1814, 3; attitude toward the war in January, 1814, 13; prosperity in 1814, 14; attitude of clergy, 21–23; banks maintain specie payments, 214; frauds in militia system of, 219; practically independent in September, 1814, 222 (see New England Convention); congressional elections of November, 1814, in, 228; effect of sedition on Madison, 231; furnishes thirteen regiments, 235; supplies Scott's brigade, 236; supplies Blakeley's crew, 237; burden of taxation thrown on, 257; probable consequence of her proposed action, 318; delighted by news of peace, ix. 59, 60; disastrous effects of peace on, 95–103, 126; church of, in 1816, 133; representatives of, oppose internal improvements, 150, 151; increase of population in 1817, 154, 155; increase of wealth in, 157–160; division of church in, 175–187. (See Massachusetts, Connecticut, etc.)

New England Confederation, tendency to, iv. 403.

New England Convention, project of, in 1804, ii. 162–188; in 1808, iv. 239, 246, 402–407; in 1812, vi. 402; in 1814, viii. 4–13; project realized in October, 1814, 225, 287; Massachusetts delegates to, 226, 227, 290–292; Rhode Island and Con-

147, 152; gives warning of embargo, 201; moves that the war-debate be public, 227; opposes enlistment of minors, 435; opposes forfeitures, 443; his Resolution on the "Hornet's" victory, vii. 65, 66; viii. 1; his opinion on the temper of Massachusetts, 223; on the Boston "Anthology," ix. 201.

RAISIN, River, defeat and massacre at the, vii. 88–97, 100.
Rambouillet, Decree of (see Decrees).
"Ramillies," Sir Thomas Hardy's flagship, viii. 94.
Ramsay, David, i. 151.
Randolph, Edmund, Burr's counsel, iii. 444.
Randolph, John, i. 143, 209; in favor of anti-Federal declarations, 260, 267, 296, 338; demands papers relating to the right of deposit at New Orleans, 429; ii. 95; defends the Louisiana treaty in Congress, 97; defends the Louisiana legislation, 120, 124; favors abolition of the Vice-Presidency, 133; favors impeachments, 142, 144; impeaches Judge Chase, 151; opposes remission of duties on school-books, 208; decline of his influence, 210; on the Yazoo claims, 210; his violent temper, 213; supported by the Administration, 220; opens the trial of Judge Chase, 229; his closing speech, 236; his amendment to the Constitution, 240, 241; asserts title to West Florida, 255; iii. 163; complains of Jefferson's credulity, ii. 409; his attitude in 1805, iii. 3, 20, 23; his antipathy to Madison, 119, 120, 126; his reception of Jefferson's secret Spanish message, 132; his war on Madison, 134; opposes Jefferson's plan of buying Florida, 136; favors an

embargo, 149; opposition of, 154; his speech against the Non-importation Resolution of Gregg, 158; attacks the Administration, 159; his account of the Mobile Act, 163; goes formally into opposition, 164; philippics against the government, 172 et seq.; his resolutions against the union of civil and military powers, 175; makes public Jefferson's secret message, 179; his dislike to Robert and Samuel Smith, 180; his schemes to reduce the revenue, 182; his object to make Madison contemptible, 182; writes to Monroe respecting Burr, 333; moves a resolution of inquiry, 335; his dictatorial tone in Congress, 349; favors abandoning New York in case of attack, 351; attacks the coastwise prohibition of slave-trade, 364; his qualities and faults, 367; his influence destroyed, 368; foreman of the jury in Burr's trial, 448; desires to indict Wilkinson, 457; his letters to Nicholson, 457; calls Jefferson's proclamation in the "Chesapeake" affair an apology, iv. 32; upholds Monroe, 129; fails to be reappointed on the Ways and Means Comm'ttee by Speaker Varnum, 153; advocates and then denounces the embargo, 174; opposes Jefferson's request for an increase of the regular army, 215, 374; his speech on war 380; discord his object, 438; claims to have prevented war, 451; his opinion of Jefferson's second administration, 454; his remarks on Jefferson. v. 78; on Erskine's arrangement, 79; on Madison's message, 177; his attempt to reduce expenditures in 1810, 199–207; on the incapacity of government, 209; on the contract with Napoleon, 344, 345; his quarrel with Eppes,

of, 89; trade with, prohibited by act of Congress, 141; character of the act, 142; Southern reasons for approving, 142.

"St. Lawrence," British line-of-battle ship, on Lake Ontario, viii. 93.

St. Lawrence River, strategic importance of, vii. 144-147; Wilkinson's expedition down, 178-191; difficulties of transport on, viii. 92; both banks to be Canadian, ix. 7, 10, 31.

St. Mary's, seized by British, ix. 62.

St. Mary's River, v. 165.

Salaberry (see De Salaberry).

Salaries of cabinet officers, vii. 398; of public officials, ix. 119-122.

Salt, repeal of duty on, iii. 182, 183; vi. 149, 150; tax to be re-enacted, 157, 166, 167.

"San Domingo," British ship-of-the-line, vii. 272.

Sandusky River, base of Harrison's campaigns, vii. 76, 78, 79, 84, 108, 109. (See Fort Stephenson.)

Sandwich, opposite Detroit, vi. 302; occupied by Harrison, vii. 132.

Saratoga, i. 92; Armstrong's idea of renewing the scene of, vii. 173; viii. 101.

"Saratoga," Macdonough's flag-ship on Lake Champlain, viii. 104; her armament, 105; in the battle of Plattsburg, 107-110; her losses, 111; ix. 234.

Sargent, Daniel, iv. 413.

Sassafras River, in Maryland, Cockburn's expedition to, vii. 268; Sir Peter Parker stationed off, viii. 165.

Sauvé, Pierre, ii. 401, 406; iii. 301.

Savannah, threatened by British, ix. 63.

Savary, Duc de Rovigo, v. 241.

Sawyer, British vice-admiral, vi. 368.

Sawyer, Lemuel, member of Congress from North Carolina, v. 184.

Scheldt, British expedition to, v. 107.

Schooner, the swiftest sailer in the world, vi. 48; privateer, vii. 315, 316; a wonderful invention, 319, 320; ix. 228, 236; the triumph of the war. vii. 322, 323.

Schuylers of New York, the. i. 108.

Scott, ———, British colonel of the Hundred-and-third Regiment, at Lundy's Lane, viii. 50; leads assault on Fort Erie, 72, 75; killed, 76. 78.

Scott, Charles, governor of Kentucky, vii. 73.

Scott, Dred, case of. ii 126, 129.

Scott, Michael, author of "Tom Cringle's Log," vii. 321; his remarks on Yankee sailors and schooners, 321-323.

Scott, Walter, i. 126; ix. 212.

Scott, Sir William, his judgments in admiralty cases, ii. 327; his judgment in the case of the "Essex," iii. 44, 45, 47; news of judgment received in America, 95, 96; opposes reforms in his court, iv. 96; his remarks on the right of retaliation, 321; decides the French decrees to be still in force, vi. 267.

Scott, Winfield, captain of artillery in 1808, vi. 292; his description of the army, 292; lieutenant-colonel at Queenston Heights, 351; surrenders, 352; colonel of Second U. S. artillery, chief-of-staff to Dearborn, vii. 156, 161; captures Fort George, 157, 158; his opinion of Wilkinson, 173; his opinion of Hampton, 174; his opinion of Brown, 409; promoted to brigadier, 409; drills his brigade at Buffalo, viii. 28, 36; organization and strength of his brigade, 35; lands below Fort Erie, 39; marches on Chippawa, 39, 40; fights the battle of Chippawa, 41-45; ordered to march toward Queenston, 50; at-

Smith, Nathaniel, delegate to the Hartford Convention, viii. 294.

Smith, Robert, appointed Secretary of the Navy, i. 220 *et seq.*; promises economies, 272; dissuades Jefferson from proposing constitutional amendment, ii. 83; consents to reduction of navy estimates, 136 ; *homme fort poli*, 373, 374; uncle of Mrs. Jerome Bonaparte, 377–379 ; a gentleman and a soldier, 431; asks to be made attorney-general, January, 1805, appointed and commissioned as attorney-general, but continues Secretary of the Navy, iii. 10–12; his opinion on Monroe's Spanish negotiation, 68; his letter to Jefferson on Burr's conspiracy, 331; wishes a call of the Senate to consider Monroe's treaty, 432; acts as Jefferson's intermediator with Rose, iv. 188–191; talks freely with Rose, 197; dislikes the embargo, 261; his opinions reported by Erskine, 384; regarded as extravagant by Gallatin, 425, 428 ; offered the Treasury Department, v. 7, 379; becomes Secretary of State, 8, 10; his language about war with France, 35; his letter to Erskine accepting settlement of the "Chesapeake" affair, 68, 69, 89; his replies to Canning's three conditions, 71–73; his remarks to Turreau on Jefferson's weakness and indiscretions, 84; introduces F. J. Jackson to the President, 120; his interviews with Jackson, 122–124, 126 ; his incompetence, 159; Madison's resentment of his conduct on Macon's bill, 186, 187; his supposed quarrels in the Cabinet, 188; opposed to Madison's course toward France, 296, 297, 366, 374, 375, 376; notifies Turreau of the President's intention to revive the non-intercourse against England, 302, 303 ; explains to Turreau the occupation of West Florida, 313; his first interviews with Serurier, 340, 347; irritates Madison by questioning Serurier, 350 ; his abilities, 363, 376 ; his removal from the State Department, 375–377 ; his Address to the People, 378; his retort against Madison, 379; Serurier's estimate of, vi. 46–50; his remark about American schooners, 48; his comments on Jefferson, Madison, and Clinton, 48; his pamphlet reveals secrets annoying to Madison, 54.

Smith, Samuel, member of Congress from Maryland, appointed temporarily Secretary of the Navy, i. 219, 245; his character, 267; moves to purchase Louisiana, 433; his vote on Chase's impeachment, ii. 238; his wish to be minister to Paris, 378; senator from Maryland, iii. 83, 126; his Non-importation Resolutions, 146, 150, 151; his wish for diplomatic office, 152, 153; his opposition to Armstrong's appointment defeated, 153, 172; punished by Jefferson, 168, 170; his view of the President's course, 169, 170; writes to Nicholas respecting Burr's conspiracy, 335 ; annoyed at Jefferson's ignoring the army in annual message, 348, 349; his letters to W. C. Nicholas respecting Jefferson's rejection of Monroe's treaty, 431 *et seq.*; on the embargo committee, iv. 172; his hostility to Gallatin, 425, 428; defeats Gallatin's appointment as Secretary of State, v. 4–7; his quarrel with Gallatin, 10, 11; votes for mission to Russia, 11; re-elected to the Senate, 159; his support of Giles, 180; defeats Macon's bill, 185, 192, 193; his motives, 185, 186, 187, 192 ; re-